LITERATURES
OF THE
AMERICAN INDIAN

LITERATURES
OF THE
AMERICAN INDIAN

A. LaVonne Brown Ruoff
University of Illinois at Chicago

Frank W. Porter III
General Editor

CHELSEA HOUSE PUBLISHERS
New York   Philadelphia

Frontispiece   A Kiowa buffalo hunter drawn by Al Momaday. The illustration appears in N. Scott Momaday's account of Kiowa history, *The Way to Rainy Mountain*.

On the cover   An 11½-inch-high Pueblo storyteller figurine modeled in clay by Cochiti potter Helen Cordero in 1969–70.

Chelsea House Publishers
Editor-in-Chief   Remmel Nunn
Managing Editor   Karyn Gullen Browne
Copy Chief   Juliann Barbato
Picture Editor   Adrian G. Allen
Art Director   Maria Epes
Deputy Copy Chief   Mark Rifkin
Assistant Art Director   Noreen Romano
Manufacturing Manager   Gerald Levine
Systems Manager   Lindsey Ottman
Production Manager   Joseph Romano
Production Coordinator   Marie Claire Cebrián

Indians of North America
Senior Editor   Liz Sonneborn

Staff for **LITERATURES OF THE AMERICAN INDIAN**
Copy Editor   Karen Hammonds
Editorial Assistant   Michele Haddad
Designer   Debora Smith
Picture Researcher   Alan Gottlieb, Sandy Jones

5   7   9   8   6   4

Library of Congress Cataloging-in-Publication Data

Ruoff, A. LaVonne Brown
Literatures of the American Indian/by A. LaVonne Brown Ruoff.
p.   cm.—(Indians of North America)
Includes bibliographical references and index.
Summary: Examines the history, evolution, and culture of the American Indians, discussing both oral and written literature.
ISBN 1-55546-688-5
      0-7910-0370-1 (pbk.)
1. Indians of North America—History. 2. Indians of North America—Social life and customs.   [1. Indians of North America—Social life and customs. 2. Indians of North America—History.] I. Title II. Series: Indians of North America (Chelsea House Publishers)   90-44893
E77.4.R96 1991   CIP
973'.0497—dc20   AC

CONTENTS

INDIANS OF NORTH AMERICA

CHELSEA HOUSE PUBLISHERS

INDIANS OF NORTH AMERICA: CONFLICT AND SURVIVAL

Frank W. Porter III

> *The Indians survived our open intention of wiping them out, and since the tide turned they have even weathered our good intentions toward them, which can be much more deadly.*
>
> John Steinbeck
> *America and Americans*

When Europeans first reached the North American continent, they found hundreds of tribes occupying a vast and rich country. The newcomers quickly recognized the wealth of natural resources. They were not, however, so quick or willing to recognize the spiritual, cultural, and intellectual riches of the people they called Indians.

The Indians of North America examines the problems that develop when people with different cultures come together. For American Indians, the consequences of their interaction with non-Indian people have been both productive and tragic. The Europeans believed they had "discovered" a "New World," but their religious bigotry, cultural bias, and materialistic world view kept them from appreciating and understanding the people who lived in it. All too often they attempted to change the way of life of the indigenous people. The Spanish conquistadores wanted the Indians as a source of labor. The Christian missionaries, many of whom were English, viewed them as potential converts. French traders and trappers used the Indians as a means to obtain pelts. As Francis Parkman, the 19th-century historian, stated, "Spanish civilization crushed the Indian; English civilization scorned and neglected him; French civilization embraced and cherished him."

7

Nearly 500 years later, many people think of American Indians as curious vestiges of a distant past, waging a futile war to survive in a Space Age society. Even today, our understanding of the history and culture of American Indians is too often derived from unsympathetic, culturally biased, and inaccurate reports. The American Indian, described and portrayed in thousands of movies, television programs, books, articles, and government studies, has either been raised to the status of the "noble savage" or disparaged as the "wild Indian" who resisted the westward expansion of the American frontier.

Where in this popular view are the real Indians, the human beings and communities whose ancestors can be traced back to ice-age hunters? Where are the creative and indomitable people whose sophisticated technologies used the natural resources to ensure their survival, whose military skill might even have prevented European settlement of North America if not for devastating epidemics and disruption of the ecology? Where are the men and women who are today diligently struggling to assert their legal rights and express once again the value of their heritage?

The various Indian tribes of North America, like people everywhere, have a history that includes population expansion, adaptation to a range of regional environments, trade across wide networks, internal strife, and warfare. This was the reality. Europeans justified their conquests, however, by creating a mythical image of the New World and its native people. In this myth, the New World was a virgin land, waiting for the Europeans. The arrival of Christopher Columbus ended a timeless primitiveness for the original inhabitants.

Also part of this myth was the debate over the origins of the American Indians. Fantastic and diverse answers were proposed by the early explorers, missionairies, and settlers. Some thought that the Indians were descended from the Ten Lost Tribes of Israel, others that they were descended from inhabitants of the lost continent of Atlantis. One writer suggested that the Indians had reached North America in another Noah's ark.

A later myth, perpetrated by many historians, focused on the relentless persecution during the past five centuries until only a scattering of these "primitive" people remained to be herded onto reservations. This view fails to chronicle the overt and covert ways in which the Indians successfully coped with the intruders.

All of these myths presented one-sided interpretations that ignored the complexity of European and American events and policies. All left serious questions unanswered. What were the origins of the American Indians? Where did they come from? How and when did they get to the New World? What was their life—their culture—really like?

In the late 1800s, anthropologists and archaeologists in the Smithsonian Institution's newly created Bureau of American Ethnology in Washington,

D.C., began to study scientifically the history and culture of the Indians of North America. They were motivated by an honest belief that the Indians were on the verge of extinction and that along with them would vanish their languages, religious beliefs, technology, myths, and legends. These men and women went out to visit, study, and record data from as many Indian communities as possible before this information was forever lost.

By this time there was a new myth in the national consciousness. American Indians existed as figures in the American past. They had performed a historical mission. They had challenged white settlers who trekked across the continent. Once conquered, however, they were supposed to accept graciously the way of life of their conquerors.

The reality again was different. American Indians resisted both actively and passively. They refused to lose their unique identity, to be assimilated into white society. Many whites viewed the Indians not only as members of a conquered nation but also as "inferior" and "unequal." The rights of the Indians could be expanded, contracted, or modified as the conquerors saw fit. In every generation, white society asked itself what to do with the American Indians. Their answers have resulted in the twists and turns of federal Indian policy.

There were two general approaches. One way was to raise the Indians to a "higher level" by "civilizing" them. Zealous missionaries considered it their Christian duty to elevate the Indian through conversion and scanty education. The other approach was to ignore the Indians until they disappeared under pressure from the ever-expanding white society. The myth of the "vanishing Indian" gave stronger support to the latter option, helping to justify the taking of the Indians' land.

Prior to the end of the 18th century, there was no national policy on Indians simply because the American nation had not yet come into existence. American Indians similarly did not possess a political or social unity with which to confront the various Europeans. They were not homogeneous. Rather, they were loosely formed bands and tribes, speaking nearly 300 languages and thousands of dialects. The collective identity felt by Indians today is a result of their common experiences of defeat and/or mistreatment at the hands of whites.

During the colonial period, the British crown did not have a coordinated policy toward the Indians of North America. Specific tribes (most notably the Iroquois and the Cherokee) became military and political pawns used by both the crown and the individual colonies. The success of the American Revolution brought no immediate change. When the United States acquired new territory from France and Mexico in the early 19th century, the federal government wanted to open this land to settlement by homesteaders. But the Indian tribes that lived on this land had signed treaties with European governments assuring their title to the land. Now the United States assumed legal responsibility for honoring these treaties.

At first, President Thomas Jefferson believed that the Louisiana Purchase contained sufficient land for both the Indians and the white population. Within a generation, though, it became clear that the Indians would not be allowed to remain. In the 1830s the federal government began to coerce the eastern tribes to sign treaties agreeing to relinquish their ancestral land and move west of the Mississippi River. Whenever these negotiations failed, President Andrew Jackson used the military to remove the Indians. The southeastern tribes, promised food and transportation during their removal to the West, were instead forced to walk the "Trail of Tears." More than 4,000 men, woman, and children died during this forced march. The "removal policy" was successful in opening the land to homesteaders, but it created enormous hardships for the Indians.

By 1871 most of the tribes in the United States had signed treaties ceding most or all of their ancestral land in exchange for reservations and welfare. The treaty terms were intended to bind both parties for all time. But in the General Allotment Act of 1887, the federal government changed its policy again. Now the goal was to make tribal members into individual landowners and farmers, encouraging their absorption into white society. This policy was advantageous to whites who were eager to acquire Indian land, but it proved disastrous for the Indians. One hundred thirty-eight million acres of reservation land were subdivided into tracts of 160, 80, or as little as 40 acres, and allotted tribe members on an individual basis. Land owned in this way was said to have "trust status" and could not be sold. But the surplus land—all Indian land not allotted to individuals—was opened (for sale) to white settlers. Ultimately, more than 90 million acres of land were taken from the Indians by legal and illegal means.

The resulting loss of land was a catastrophe for the Indians. It was necessary to make it illegal for Indians to sell their land to non-Indians. The Indian Reorganization Act of 1934 officially ended the allotment period. Tribes that voted to accept the provisions of this act were reorganized, and an effort was made to purchase land within preexisting reservations to restore an adequate land base.

Ten years later, in 1944, federal Indian policy again shifted. Now the federal government wanted to get out of the "Indian business." In 1953 an act of Congress named specific tribes whose trust status was to be ended "at the earliest possible time." This new law enabled the United States to end unilaterally, whether the Indians wished it or not, the special status that protected the land in Indian tribal reservations. In the 1950s federal Indian policy was to transfer federal responsibility and jurisdiction to state governments, encourage the physical relocation of Indian peoples from reservations to urban areas, and hasten the termination, or extinction, of tribes.

Between 1954 and 1962 Congress passed specific laws authorizing the termination of more than 100 tribal groups. The stated purpose of the termination policy was to ensure the full and complete integration of Indians into American society. However, there is a less benign way to interpret this legislation. Even as termination was being discussed in Congress, 133 separate bills were introduced to permit the transfer of trust land ownership from Indians to non-Indians.

With the Johnson administration in the 1960s the federal government began to reject termination. In the 1970s yet another Indian policy emerged. Known as "self-determination," it favored keeping the protective role of the federal government while increasing tribal participation in, and control of, important areas of local government. In 1983 President Reagan, in a policy statement on Indian affairs, restated the unique "government is government" relationship of the United States with the Indians. However, federal programs since then have moved toward transferring Indian affairs to individual states, which have long desired to gain control of Indian land and resources.

As long as American Indians retain power, land, and resources that are coveted by the states and the federal government, there will continue to be a "clash of cultures," and the issues will be contested in the courts, Congress, the White House, and even in the international human rights community. To give all Americans a greater comprehension of the issues and conflicts involving American Indians today is a major goal of this series. These issues are not easily understood, nor can these conflicts be readily resolved. The study of North American Indian history and culture is a necessary and important step toward that comprehension. All Americans must learn the history of the relations between the Indians and the federal government, recognize the unique legal status of the Indians, and understand the heritage and cultures of the Indians of North America.

Mountain Chief, a Blackfoot Indian, interprets a tribal song recorded on a phonographic cylinder for ethnologist Frances Densmore, 1916. Densmore was one of the first and most prolific recorders and translators of American Indian music.

THE
FIRST
AMERICAN LITERATURE

American literature begins with the first human perception of the American landscape expressed and preserved in language.
—N. Scott Momaday, "The Native Voice"

The writings of 17th-century English colonists are often said to be the first works of American literature. But by the time authors such as John Smith and Anne Bradstreet wrote of their experiences in North America, the continent already had a 28,000-year literary history. Its creators were North America's native inhabitants, the peoples whom early European explorers collectively referred to as Indians.

When Europeans first began to immigrate to North America in the late 16th and early 17th centuries, the total Indian population was approximately 18 million, 5 million of whom lived in what is now the United States. Far from being one people, they belonged to more than 300 different cultural groups and spoke approximately 200 languages, about 150 of which survive in the 20th century. The cultural beliefs, social structures, and ways of life of these Indian groups varied greatly, a diversity reflected in the rich treasury of their literatures. Although individual Indians now vary in the extent to which they follow tribal traditions, their worldviews and values still have much in common with those of their ancestors. These perspectives continue to help shape the works created by American Indian authors today.

In this book, the term *literature* refers to both oral and written works. Some Indian groups recorded their literatures in written form prior to contact with non-Indians. For example, the rituals of the Ojibwa were preserved in pictures (called pictographs by anthropologists) drawn on birch-bark scrolls. But most traditional Indian literature was communicated verbally. This oral literature—sometimes called *verbal arts* or *folklore*—included songs, stories, and ritual dramas (ceremonies). Only in the 20th century did most new literary works produced by Indians take written form. Particularly since the late 1960s, increasing numbers of American Indians have become highly acclaimed novelists and poets. Even today, however, American Indians continue to create and perform the oral literatures that strongly influence the written works of contemporary Indian authors. In the words of Acoma poet Simon Ortiz,

The oral tradition is not just speaking and listening, because what it means to me and to other people who have grown up in that tradition is that whole process, . . . of that society in terms of its history, its culture, its language, its values, and subsequently, its literature. So it is not merely a simple matter of speaking and listening, but living that process.

American Indian oral literatures are performed arts. Over time, a general structure for a traditional ceremony, myth, or song tends to be established by a tribe. But within that structure, a ceremonialist, storyteller, or singer is usually permitted some leeway to create his or her own interpretation. As long as the interpretations are accepted by the group as true to the spirit and content of the original, are performed appropriately, and achieve the desired result, many tribes consider each performer's version as valid. The changes performers may make include revising the work by adding allusions to recent events, using the pitch of their voice or gestures to dramatize its contents, and soliciting a response from the audience. It is common for audience members to play a role in a performance. Often a storyteller's audience is expected to say specific words, either to encourage the storyteller to begin or to continue. If the encouragement is not forthcoming, the storyteller may stop.

The degree to which improvisation is permissible may vary from one form of literature to another within a tribe. For instance, among the Papago, a storyteller spends years memorizing the complicated body of prose and verse that constitutes that tribe's "bible." Once he has mastered these works, the storyteller may embellish the prose, but he cannot do so with the verse. The Papago believe that the words and tune to all of their songs were given to them by a mythic hero named Elder Brother. Therefore, the songs are too sacred to be altered.

Even if a performer is not required to know a work word for word, performance of oral literatures can sometimes demand great feats of memory. For example, Navajo performers of the Night Chant or Nightway, a healing ritual, must learn a great body of works in order to participate in the ceremony, which takes place over eight and a half days.

Because almost every tribe's traditional ceremonies, stories, and songs survived from time immemorial only in the memory of its members, each gen-

Evening in the Lodge, *an illustration from* Indian Boyhood *by Charles Eastman. In his 1902 autobiography, Eastman explains that in traditional Sioux society children "listened with parted lips and glistening eyes" to tribal stories their elders told them nearly every evening.*

eration faces the danger of losing its ancestral oral traditions unless they are taught to the tribe's children. In *Indian Boyhood* (1902), Sioux author Charles Eastman describes how his tribe trained young boys from an early age to assume the task of preserving and transmitting its legends:

Almost every evening a myth, or a true story of some deed done in the past, was narrated by one of the parents or grandparents, while the boy listened with parted lips and glistening eyes. On the following evening he was usually required to repeat it. If he was not an apt scholar, he struggled long with his task; but, as a rule, the Indian boy was a good listener and had a good memory, so that the stories were tolerably well mastered. The household became his audience, by which he was alternately criticized and applauded.

Because oral literatures are meant to be performed, many Indians object to recording them in writing. Some groups also believe that religious ceremonies, myths, and songs are too sacred to be discussed or collected for study by people outside their tribe. But some Indians fear that their traditional oral literature will be forgotten if it is not transcribed.

This belief was shared by the many non-Indians who began to record Indians' verbal arts in the 19th century. The collection of oral literature in what is now the United States was spurred on by the publication of Henry Rowe Schoolcraft's *Algic Researches* (1839), which focused on Ojibwa culture and literature. Publishers responded to the public's interest in Schoolcraft's book by bringing out a number of Indian life histories and autobiographies, most of which included examples of oral literature. But it was not until the late 19th and early 20th centuries that anthropologists and linguists began to study systematically the elements of American Indian cultures, including literature.

Despite their good intentions, many of these scholars misrepresented the material they intended to preserve. Often they merely took down the words spoken by their informants without recording any information about the performance itself or the cultural significance of the work. The translation of oral literature from Indian languages into English also sometimes distorted the works. Some non-Indian translators used overly formal language to persuade whites that what they were recording could be considered literature. Others were so literal that their graceless translations conveyed none of the beauty of the original work. Still others molded their translations to fit their beliefs about the tribe and its culture, ideas that were oftentimes incorrect.

Recently, modern poets and critics have reworked some of these early translations to produce their own versions. On the facing page is one such translation by Larry Evers and Felipe S. Molina of a Yaqui song that was recorded in 1922 by Frances Densmore, one of the earliest and most prolific re-

LITTLE RED [QUAIL]
from the Yaqui Deer Songs

Little red [quail],
  walking afar where there is no water,
    where do they make the kukupopoti sound?
Little red [quail],
  walking afar where there is no water,
    where do they make the kukupopoti sound?

Over here, in the center
  of the flower-covered wilderness,
    walking afar where there is no water,
      where do they make the kukupopoti sound?
Little red [quail],
  walking afar where there is no water,
    where do they make the kukupopoti sound?

corders of American Indian music. Densmore had paraphrased the content of this song as "The quail in the bush is making his sound [whirring]." As Evers and Molina's translation makes evident, this paraphrase omits the line and stanza structure, action, representation of the sound of the quail, and other features of the song that contribute to its beauty.

In addition to the large body of oral literatures that survives and continues to be performed today, American Indian literatures also include works written in English by Native American authors since the late 18th century. Primarily written to explain Indian culture and history to non-Indians, these works often combine the themes and forms of traditional Indian oral literatures with genres used by Western European writers. Because the written literature often incorporates the songs, myths, and ceremonies as well as tribal beliefs, history, and customs, readers can most fully appreciate this literature by learning about the cultures that the authors describe. Although the hundreds of Indian groups in the United States have historically had different ways of life, some generalizations can be made about the Indian's view of the universe and how this perspective manifests itself in Indian literatures.

One dominant theme in both oral and written works is the belief that human beings must live in harmony with the physical and spiritual universe. Such harmony may be achieved through the power of thought and the power of word. As employed in religious rituals, thought and word can bring rain, enrich a harvest, provide good hunting, heal physical and mental sickness, maintain good relations among people within a group, bring victory against an enemy, win a loved one, or ward off evil spirits. Because of the great power of thought and word, Indian people feel both should be used with great care. Otherwise, the thoughts people have or the words they speak might in some way hurt them.

The power of thought and word to create is beautifully demonstrated by poet and novelist Leslie Marmon Silko (Laguna) in her introduction to her 1977 novel *Ceremony*. In the following passage, Silko describes how the Laguna Indians' creator thought the universe into existence:

> Ts'its'tsi'nako, Thought-Woman
> is sitting in her room
> and whatever she thinks about
> appears.
>
> . . . .
>
> Thought-Woman, the spider,
> named things and
> as she named them
> they appeared.
>
> She is sitting in her room
> thinking of a story now
>
> I am telling you the story
> she is thinking.

Coupled with the power of the word is the power of silence. Alluding to this power, Kiowa novelist N. Scott Momaday has called silence "the dimension in which ordinary and extraordinary events take their proper places." For example, in certain circumstances, the Western Apache decide to "give up on words" as a means of communicating with other people. They choose to remain silent during such diverse situations as meeting strangers, being with a loved one during the initial stages of courtship, and being with someone who is verbally attacking them.

Another basic theme in American Indians' oral and written literatures is the peoples' deep reverence for the land. The traditional accounts of a tribe's origin and history often include

A tribe's traditional narratives sometimes describe the creation or history of a geological landmark in the group's homeland. For instance, Navajo myth holds that the top of Shiprock, an isolated mountain in northwestern New Mexico, was long ago the home of a monstrous bird that was killed by twin sons of the sun.

references to specific places in its homeland, thereby giving these places a sense of sacredness. Recent American Indian authors continue to emphasize in their writings the importance of place. In *The Way to Rainy Mountain*, Momaday movingly describes the significance of land to him in this way:

Once in his life a man ought to concentrate his mind upon the remembered earth, I believe. He ought to give himself up to a particular landscape in his experience, to look at it from as many angles as he can, to wonder about it, dwell upon it. He ought to imagine that he touches it with his hands at every season and listens to the sounds that are made upon it. He ought to imagine the creatures that are there and all the faintest motions of the wind. He ought to recollect the glare of noon and all the colors of dawn and dusk.

Linked to reverence for the land is an emphasis on direction. The number four is frequently incorporated into the content and form of Indian literary works because many tribes consider the number sacred, as it represents the cardinal directions (north, south, east, and west) as well as the seasons and stages of human life (infancy, childhood, adulthood, and old age). Multiples of four and six, the latter of which is used to represent the cardinal directions and the directions above and below the earth, are also common.

Circularity is also emphasized in Indian literatures. The circle symbolizes the sun and its circuit. In addition, it sometimes represents the cycle and continuum of human life. In his 1932 autobiography, a Sioux medicine man named Black Elk describes the importance of the circle to his tribe as follows:

You have noticed that everything an Indian does is in a circle, and that is because the Power of the World always works in circles, and everything tries to be round. In the old days when we were a strong and happy people, all our power came to us from the sacred hoop of the nation, and so long as the hoop was unbroken, the people flourished. The flowering tree was the living center of the hoop, and the circle of the four quarters nourished it. The east gave peace and light, the south gave warmth, the west gave rain, and the north with its cold and mighty wind gave strength and endurance. This knowledge came to us from the outer world with our religion. Everything the Power of the World does is done in a circle. The sky is round, and I have heard that the earth is round like a ball, and so are the stars. The wind, in its greatest power, whirls. Birds make their nests in circles, for theirs is the same religion as ours. The sun comes forth and goes down again in a circle. The moon does the same, and both are round. Even the seasons form a great circle in their changing, and always come back again to where they were. The life of a man is a circle from childhood to childhood, and so it is, in everything where power moves. Our tepees were round like the nests of birds, and these were always set in a circle, the nation's hoop, a nest of many nests, where the Great Spirit meant for us to hatch our children.

The importance of the circle is also reflected in many American Indian ceremonies and dances. Among the Mescalero Apache, for example, girls at puberty perform a ceremony during which they run around a basket four times, providing a visual reminder of the cycle of life. In addition, the structures of traditional Indian narratives are often cyclical. For instance, the narratives sometimes tell of a mythic hero or heroine who leaves a community only to return after many trials and adventures.

Also found in Indians' literary works is a strong sense of community. Tribal literatures often stress the need for cooperation and good relations among the people within a group. Generosity, helpfulness, and respect for age and experience are virtues that are highly valued by many tribes for these qualities have enabled them to survive over time. Ella C. Deloria, a Dakota Sioux, comments in *Speaking of Indians* (1944) that her people "understand the meaning of self-sacrifice, perhaps because their legends taught them that the buffalo, on which their very life depended, gave itself voluntarily that they might live." The following Keres song also communicates the desire of Indian individuals to feel at one with the other members of their community:

I add my breath to your breath
That our days may be long on the Earth
That the days of our people may be long
That we may be one person
That we may finish our roads together
May our mother bless you with life
May our Life Paths be fulfilled.

Native Americans have always had a strong oral tradition of creative writing. As they mastered the written word, they used it to preserve their oral traditions and to create new written ones in genres that were not part of traditional Indian culture. Their oral and written works reveal the rich imaginations and wealth of perspectives of the peoples who are the original inhabitants of what is now the United States. Only with knowledge of their literatures can the true literary heritage of the United States be appreciated. ▲

A group of Kiowa Indians makes recordings of their traditional songs as Commissioner of Indian Affairs John C. Collier looks on, 1939. During his tenure as commissioner, Collier initiated a variety of federal programs aimed at preserving Indian cultures.

CEREMONY
AND
SONG

The methods tribes and scholars use to categorize oral literatures vary considerably. Indians often have their own distinctive terms to identify genres, which usually do not correspond to those of European and American literature. However, for convenience' sake, works of American Indian oral literature are divided into the following categories in this book: ritual dramas, songs, narratives, speeches, and life histories. Ritual dramas and songs will be discussed in this chapter; narratives, in Chapter 3; and speeches and life histories, in Chapter 4.

Because it combines song, narrative, and oratory, the most complex form of oral literature is the ritual drama. (*Ritual drama* is the term most commonly used by scholars to refer to what Indian people usually call chants, chantways, ceremonies, or rituals.) American Indians use ritual dramas to order their spiritual and physical world.

The tool for creating this order is the power of word, whether it is chanted, spoken, or sung. A tribe often has special words or even entire languages that are used only when performing ceremonies. For instance, the Sioux Indians have two types of sacred language: *wakan iye* and *hanbloblaka*. The former is used among medicine men; the latter is used by medicine men to communicate with spirit helpers.

Ritual dramas always have a well-defined structure. All parts must be performed in a particular sequence if the ceremony is to achieve the desired effect. The specific goals of ritual dramas vary. Among farming peoples, rituals are often performed seasonally to ensure a good harvest or to renew the earth's fertility before planting. Some ceremonies are held to protect a tribe from any contamination from outside forces. For instance, many tribes traditionally performed purification rituals when a tribal member was returned to the people's homeland after being held captive by another Indian group. More recently, some southwestern tribes have conducted rituals to purify veterans of World War II, the Korean War, and the Vietnam War. Ritual dramas may also be held to mark an important occasion in an individual's life, such as the receipt of a name, the onset of puberty, marriage, and death.

Although many people participate in ceremonies, only special individuals may oversee them. In some tribes, especially those that are settled farmers, these people are known as priests or singers. Their status is usually inherited, although they must serve an apprenticeship with established priests in order to learn the complexities of the rituals they hope to master. Among peoples whose food supply comes primarily from hunting and gathering wild plants, ritual leaders are usually known as shamans. Unlike priests, shamans can perform ceremonies only after they have been inspired by a vision. Groups of people who belong to special religious societies also conduct rituals in some tribes. For example, among the Ojibwa, Menominee, and Winnebago, the members of the Midéwiwin, or Grand Medicine Society, carry out healing rituals.

An example of a southwestern ritual drama is the Navajo Night Chant, or Nightway. The purpose of the Night Chant is to cure the mind and body of an ill tribal member. But the ceremony also acts to unite a community as the many participants and spectators work together to achieve a cure.

The ceremony begins at sunset and ends at sunrise eight and a half days later. During the first four days, the patient is purified by having corn pollen applied to his or her body and by taking sweat baths. The gods awake at midnight of the fourth day and descend to earth. There, they appear in sand paintings—holy images formed by a priest from pulverized minerals and crushed charcoal. The Navajo believe that when corn pollen is sprinkled on the painting by the singer and the one for whom a ceremony is being performed, the holy people become present in the sand painting. In a sand-painting rite, the sick person walks onto and sits in the middle of the painting, where he or she is identified with each of the holy people present in it. The sands are taken from the feet, legs, body, and head of each of the sand-painted figures and pressed onto the corresponding body parts of the person sitting on the sand painting. When this identification is complete, the sand painting is destroyed by the singer, and the mixed sands are removed and ritually returned to nature. The Night Chant comes to a climax on the ninth day. All of the songs performed the previous eight days are sung throughout the night. The ceremony concludes at sunrise when the healed patient faces east and inhales the breath of dawn, making him or her ready to begin life anew.

The Night Chant includes large numbers of prayers and songs. One of

Three men dressed in masks, collars, and head ornaments worn by participants in the Navajo ritual drama known as the Night Chant.

the best known is the prayer spoken by the chanter on the morning of the third day—the day of the west. Mentioned in the prayer is the house made of dawn (called Tsegíhi in the Navajo language), a shrine in the Canyon de Chelly in northeastern Arizona in the center of the Navajo homeland. It is a two-story cliff house built of yellow sandstone, whose upper portion is painted white and whose lower, unpainted portion is yellow. In Navajo symbolism, white is the color of the east and yellow is that of the west. The upper story is sacred

to the Hastshéyalti, or Talking God, who is the god of dawn and the east. The lower is sacred to the Hasthého-gan, or House God, who is god of west and evening twilight. The prayer illustrates the emphasis on physical and spiritual harmony and on the sacredness of place that is so often a part of American Indian oral literatures. Other common elements are the use of repetition, comprehensive allusions to nature, and description of a progression from physical well-being to spiritual peace to the ability to speak.

A Navajo man making a sand painting from pulverized sandstone and charcoal. This sand painting was used during a 1954 ceremony to help heal a sick child.

Tsegíhi!
House made of dawn.
House made of evening light.
House made of the dark cloud.
House made of dark mist.
House made of female rain.
House made of pollen.
House made of grasshoppers.
Dark cloud is at the door.
The trail out of it is dark cloud.
The zigzag lightning stands high upon it.
Male deity!
Your offering I make.
I have prepared a smoke for you.
Restore my feet for me.
Restore my legs for me.
Restore my body for me.
Restore my mind for me.
Restore my voice for me.
This very day take out your spell for me.
Your spell remove for me.
You have taken it away for me.
Far off it has gone.
Happily I recover.
Happily my interior becomes cool.
Happily I go forth.
My interior feeling cold, may I walk.
No longer sore, may I walk.
Impervious to pain, may I walk.
With lively feelings, may I walk.
As it used to be long ago, may I walk.
Happily may I walk.
Happily with abundant dark clouds may I
    walk.
Happily with abundant showers may I
    walk.
Happily with abundant plants may I
    walk.
Happily on a trail of pollen may I walk.
Happily may I walk.
Being as it used to be long ago, may I
    walk.

May it be beautiful before me.
May it be beautiful behind me.
May it be beautiful below me.
May it be beautiful all around me.
In beauty it is finished.
In beauty it is finished.

One of the Iroquois Indians' major healing ceremonies is the Ritual of Condolence, which is intended not to cure an individual but rather to heal society as a whole. It is held after the death of one of the chiefs of the council of fifty, representing the Confederated Five Nations of the Iroquois.

Traditionally, there were two great divisions, or moieties, among the Iroquois: senior (Mohawk, Onondaga, Seneca) and junior (Oneida and Cayuga). Women usually married men from the other moiety, a custom that helped to integrate the group. The Ritual of Condolence is meant to unite society in a similar way. The participants are divided into two groups, who may be seen symbolically as marriage partners as they take turns performing the various parts of the ritual. At the close of the performance, the speaker asks the male participants to dance with the female participants from the other moiety, indicating that the breach in Iroquois society caused by the chief's death has been healed.

The Ritual of Condolence also recalls and reaffirms the formation of the league of Iroquois tribes, which according to legend was conceived by Hiawatha in about A.D. 1500. The confederation put an end to the tribes' vendettas, or blood feuds, with one another. These feuds arose when a person from one tribe killed someone from another. The kinsmen of the victim were bound by custom to avenge the death by killing a person from the murderer's tribe, an act that would then have to be avenged by the other group.

By disrupting the structure of the confederacy, the death of a chief is therefore seen by the Iroquois as a threat to the peace among the confederated tribes. The enemy of society is both death itself and the cult of death, which leads to despair and possible insanity. During the Ritual of Condolence, this threat is eliminated by renaming the dead chief's successor after the deceased, whose name is always the same as one of the 50 chiefs of the original Iroquois council. Thus, the dead chief as well as one of the league's founders is figuratively resurrected as the new chief.

The excerpt below is called "Within His Breast" and is the fourth article of the portion of the ritual entitled the "Requickening" (restoration of the senses and mind from the destruction of grief). It is delivered to the mourners by the Cleareyed Orator, representing the nongrieving Iroquois. The excerpt, translated in the 19th century, stresses the progressive nature of healing:

Is not what has befallen thee then so dreadful that it must not be neglected? For, at the present time, there are wrenchings without ceasing within thy breast, and also within thy mind. Now truly, the disorder now among the organs within thy breast is such that nothing can be clearly discerned. So great has been the affliction that has befallen thee that yellow spots have developed within thy body, and truly thy life forces have become greatly weakened thereby; truly thou dost now suffer.

It is, therefore, that in ancient times it thus came to pass that the hodiyaaehshon, the Federal Chiefs, our grandsires, made a formal rule, saying "Let us unite our affairs; let us formulate regulations; let us ordain this among others that what we shall prepare we will designate by the name Water-of-pity, which shall be the essential thing to be used where Death has caused this dreadful affliction, inducing bitter grief."

And so, in whatever place it may be that such a tragedy will befall a person, it shall be the duty of him whose mind is left unscathed by it to take up and make use of the Water-of-pity, so denominated by us, by taking it in hand, and then pouring it down the throat of the one on whom the great affliction has fallen; and, it shall be that when the Water-of-pity shall have permeated the inside of his body, it will at once begin the work of reorganizing all the many things there which have been disarranged and disordered by the shock of the death, not only in his body but also in his mind; and it will also remove utterly all the yellow gall spots from his throat and from the inside of his body.

Songs are a vital component of most ritual dramas. But their importance to Indians is still greater. In fact, songs are central to all aspects of American Indian life. Many tribes, such as the Ojibwa, regard singing as one of their greatest pleasures. The Papago believe that

A 1917 sketch of a turtle-shell rattle used by the Cahuilla Indians to accompany ceremonial songs.

song is a form of magic that compels the powers of nature to do man's will. Among the Inuit, the word *anerca* means both breath and poetry. Orpingalik, a Netsilik Inuit, describes his songs as "thoughts, sung out with the breath when people are moved by great forces and ordinary speech no longer suffices." With the importance placed on songs, it is not surprising that they constitute the largest part of American Indian oral literatures.

Songs are often accompanied by a percussion instrument, usually a drum or a rattle. Sometimes a whistle or a flute is used. However, the voice of the singer is always the basic instrument and provides the song's melody.

Among Indian groups, the criteria for a good singer vary. For instance, the Flathead (also known as Salish) feel that for a person to sing well, his lungs, throat, and memory must be strong. They also particularly value a high-pitched voice because it can be so penetrating. However, a voice should not be so high-pitched that it drowns out the other singers. Ojibwa songs, on the other hand, require people to sing vibrato. Mastery of this difficult technique, in which the voice has a tremulous quality, is considered a sign of musical proficiency by the tribe.

The origins of songs are likewise different from tribe to tribe. The Pima believe that many of their songs were sung at the beginning of time by the creator or other gods and then handed down by teachers. These songs are a part of their traditional legends and major ceremonies.

The Flathead hold that although some of their songs were composed by tribal members or have been borrowed from neighboring peoples, all true and proper songs originated through contact between humans and superhuman beings. The way humans learn songs from spirits always follows the same pattern. A person first hears a song faintly, as the being begins singing it from far away. Gradually, the being comes closer and closer, singing constantly, until the human has mastered the song. The Flathead believe that the more creative the hearer is, the fewer times the song will have to be repeated.

The Papago similarly believe that songs are given to them by supernatural powers. If a tribal member wants to learn a song, he must first perform an act of heroism, the greatest of which is going to war, because the Papago hold that warriors come in contact with the supernatural. After this has been done, the would-be singer must fast. Eventually, if he is deemed worthy by the spirits, he will have a vision that includes a song.

Songs are composed both communally and individually. Among the Zuni, song composition is usually communal. The members of each kiva, or underground religious house, usually include two or three composers. At gatherings, the kiva's dance chief invites them to present their songs to the group by asking them what they are "holding." A composer with a song will then sing a shortened version of it. Sometimes a song will be immediately accepted by the kiva group, but more often it is revised by the other members.

Songs are composed by individuals as well. The Tsimshian Indians honor talented composers who supply new songs for feasts and ceremonies. When planning such an event, a host engages the services of a composer. The host not only requests that he compose songs that praise the host's achievements and glorify his ancestors but also ones that

comment on the weaknesses and defects of selected guests. A composer must use subtle wordplay to make sure that his derisive songs do not directly insult the guests but nevertheless leave little doubt about the identity of their intended victim.

Hopi composers also create songs for tribal ceremonies. Although the sentiments the songs express are personal, they are meant to communicate the shared experience of the ritual's participants and are never ascribed to the composer. In some tribes, however, particular songs can be owned by an individual or family, as the following comments of a Hupa Indian make clear:

I have made two songs for the White Deer Dance. When I made them, I would go out by myself and sing them low so nobody could hear them. Then I sang them the next time there was a White Deer Dance. Then people know them; they were my songs. I would sing them again and again, when there was a White Deer Dance. People could learn them because they heard them a few times. But they could not sing them. If there was a White Deer Dance and I was not there, a relative of mine could sing them. If somebody else wanted to sing them he would have to ask me for permission, whether I am there for the dance or not.

Many Indian songs are composed to be part of ritual dramas. For example, there are several hundred songs connected with the Midéwiwin, or Grand Medicine Society, of the Ojibwa, many of which have direct ceremonial use. These songs preserve the ancient teach-

Chief Ojibway standing outside a lodge of the Midéwiwin, or Grand Medicine Society, 1910. Hundreds of Ojibwa songs are associated with the Midéwiwin.

ings and beliefs of the society. The following song, "The Sky Clears," affirms the power of the Midéwiwin over a ritual participant:

Verily
The sky clears
When my Midé drum
Sounds
For me
Verily
The waters are smooth
When my Midé drum
Sounds
For me.

Sacred songs from different tribes use many of the same techniques to express the supplication of the group. Among these are repetition, enumeration of directions and parts of the body, and incremental development, in which phrases and lines are repeated, accompanied by minor changes in the repeated positions. All three of these can be found in "Flower Wilderness World," reproduced on the next page. This song is part of the Yaqui Deer Songs that were traditionally sung by three men to accompany the perfor-

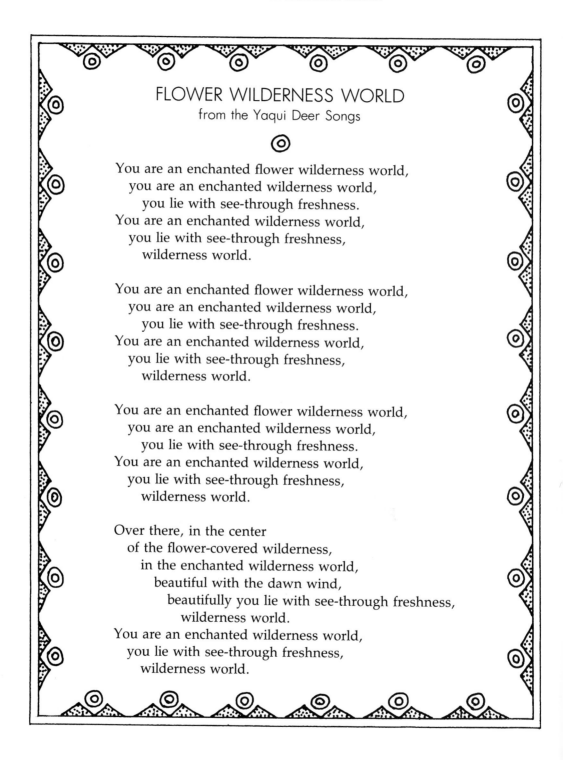

FLOWER WILDERNESS WORLD
from the Yaqui Deer Songs

You are an enchanted flower wilderness world,
  you are an enchanted wilderness world,
    you lie with see-through freshness.
You are an enchanted wilderness world,
  you lie with see-through freshness,
    wilderness world.

You are an enchanted flower wilderness world,
  you are an enchanted wilderness world,
    you lie with see-through freshness.
You are an enchanted wilderness world,
  you lie with see-through freshness,
    wilderness world.

You are an enchanted flower wilderness world,
  you are an enchanted wilderness world,
    you lie with see-through freshness.
You are an enchanted wilderness world,
  you lie with see-through freshness,
    wilderness world.

Over there, in the center
  of the flower-covered wilderness,
    in the enchanted wilderness world,
      beautiful with the dawn wind,
        beautifully you lie with see-through freshness,
      wilderness world.
You are an enchanted wilderness world,
  you lie with see-through freshness,
    wilderness world.

mance of the deer dancer. These songs describe a double world, both "here" and "over there," in which all the actions of the deer dancer have a parallel in that mythic, prehistoric place the Yaqui call *sea ania*, or flower world. The song describes the freshness of the world that the deer sees as the sun rises.

In "Song of the Sky Loom," the Tewa prayer that appears below, incremental development and repetition are used to create a metaphor, in which the daily changes in the sky are compared to the creation of woven fabric on a loom.

Some songs are a part of rituals that ensure the survival of the group. Papago planters sing the following song as they walk through their fields night after night, "singing up the corn." (In the final stanza, "crazy corn" refers to corn with kernels of two colors; "laughing corn" describes corn with kernels of three colors.)

SONG OF THE SKY LOOM
a Tewa prayer

Oh our Mother the Earth, oh our Father the Sky,
Your children are we, and with tired backs
We bring you the gifts that you love.
Then weave for us a garment of brightness;
May the warp be the white light of morning,
May the weft be the red light of evening,
May the fringes be the falling rain,
May the border be the standing rainbow.
Thus weave for us a garment of brightness
That we may walk fittingly where birds sing,
That we may walk fittingly where grass is green
Oh our Mother the Earth, oh our Father the Sky!

Evening is falling
Pleasantly sounding
Will reverberate
Our songs

The corn comes up;
It comes up green;
Here upon our fields
Green leaves blow in the breeze.

Blue evening falls,
Blue evening falls;
Near by, in every direction,
It sets the corn tassels trembling.

The wind smooths well the ground.
Yonder the wind runs
Upon our fields.
The corn leaves tremble.

On Tecolote fields
The corn is growing green.
I came there, saw the tassels waving in
    the breeze,
And I whistled softly for joy.

Blowing in the wind,
Singing,
Am I crazy corn?
Blowing in the wind,

Singing,
Am I laughing corn?

Songs are not only a part of the rituals of individual tribes but also of religious movements in which many Indian groups participate. One such movement was the Ghost Dance religion, which swept across the Great Plains in about 1890. Led by Wovoka (a.k.a. Jack Wilson), a Paiute medicine man, the movement taught that Indians would be reunited with family and friends in another world where there was no sickness, death, or old age, if they lived in peace and ended their old practices, danced themselves into trances, and avoided alcohol, quarreling among themselves, and warring with whites. By performing the Ghost Dance at intervals, each time for five successive days, believers sought to bring about this reunion and the return of the buffalo, which were rapidly dying out on the Plains at the time. The following Sioux Ghost Dance song, recorded by anthropologist James Mooney in *The Ghost Dance Religion* (1892), summarizes the hopes of the movement's followers and their belief that they would receive a message from two sacred birds—the crow, which symbolized the spirit world, and the eagle, whose feathers were used to make war bonnets:

The whole world is coming.
A nation is coming, a nation is coming,
The Eagle has brought the message to the
    tribe.
The father says so, the father says so.
Over the whole earth they are coming.
The buffalo are coming, the buffalo are
    coming.
The Crow has brought the message to the
    tribe,
The father says so, the father says so.

Arapaho Indians performing the Ghost Dance, photographed by anthropologist James Mooney in about 1893.

A unique use of song is found in the Inuit tradition of the musical duel. These duels, during which two contestants alternate singing songs the lyrics of which ridicule their opponent, serve two purposes. They are entertainment for the spectators and a means of settling disputes that threaten to disrupt the harmony of the group. Sometimes contestants use traditional songs, but often they create compositions specially designed to emphasize the dueling partner's weaknesses. The following songs are from a duel between two men, designated by the recorder of their songs as "K" and "E." K, an elderly man, had divorced his wife, who remarried E. A dispute arose between K and E when K announced he wanted his wife back.

K—
Now shall I split off words—little,
    sharp words
Like the wooden splinters which I
    hack off with my ax.
A song from ancient times—a breath
    of the ancestors
A song of longing—for my wife.
An impudent, black-skinned oaf has
    stolen her,
Has tried to belittle her.
A miserable wretch who loves
        human flesh—
A cannibal from famine days.

E—
Insolence that takes the breath away
Such laughable arrogance and effrontery.
What a satirical song! Supposed to
    place the blame on me.
You would drive fear into my heart!
I who care not about death.

Hi! You sing about my woman who
    was your wench.
You weren't so loving then—she was
    much alone.
You forgot to prize her in song,
    in stout, contest songs.
Now she is mine.
And never shall she visit singing,
    false lovers.
Betrayer of women in strange
    households.

American Indian songs may sometimes express the personal experiences of an individual. Among these are dream songs, which are especially common among Plains Indians. Young men learned dream songs from spirits in visions. In *Life, Letters and Speeches* (1851), the Ojibwa writer George Copway includes this song, which was taught to him as a youth:

It is I who travel in the winds,
It is I who whisper in the breeze,
    I shake the trees.
    I shake the earth,
I trouble the waters on every land.

Indian songs often include lyrics that express a person's feelings when in love or when experiencing sorrow or loss. The following love song reveals an Ojibwa singer's sadness at parting from her lover:

A loon
I thought it was
But it was
My love's
Splashing oar

To Sault Ste. Marie
He has departed
My love
Has gone on before me
Never again
Can I see him
[Repeat verse one]

After his surrender to U.S. authorities in 1881, Sioux chief Sitting Bull composed this moving song that expressed his sense of loss:

A warrior
I have been
now
it is all over
a hard time
I have

The Kiowa's wind songs are usually created and sung by someone at home who is thinking of a warrior at battle far away. These songs describe the loneliness and longing of people living on the open prairie, where only the sweep of the wind breaks the silence. "Maiden's Song" is an example of this genre.

Idlers and cowards are here at home now,
Whenever they wish, they see their loved
    ones.
O idlers and cowards are here at home
    now,
O idlers and cowards are here at home
    now,
But the young man I love has gone to
    war, far away.
Weary, lonely, he longs for me.

Other kinds of personal songs include women's work songs, hunting songs, elegies, and lullabies. The following Thule Inuit lullaby communicates a mother's pride in her baby boy and her feeling of contentment about her motherhood and her son's well-being.

It is my big baby
That I feel in my hood
Oh how heavy he is!
Ya ya! Ya ya!

When I turn
He smiles at me, my little one,
Well hidden in my hood,
Oh how heavy he is!
Ya ya! Ya ya!

How sweet he is when he smiles
With two teeth like a little walrus.
Ah, I like my little one to be heavy
And my hood to be full.

The Zuni sing a special song in a ritual in which they present their infants to the sun. On the eighth day of a baby's life, the women of her or his father's clan wash the infant's head and place cornmeal in the child's hand. The baby is then taken outside and held so that he or she faces the east at the moment of sunrise. Cornmeal is sprinkled toward the rising sun while the paternal grandmother says the following prayer:

We came to day.
Now this day
Our fathers,
Dawn priests,
Have come out standing to their sacred
   place.
Our sun father
Having come out standing to his sacred
   place,

Our child,
It is your day.
This day,
The flesh of the white corn,
Prayer meal,
To our sun father
This prayer meal we offer.
May your road be fulfilled
Reading to the road of your sun father.
We offer prayer meal.
To this end:
May you help us all to finish our roads.

In addition to ritual and personal songs, there are songs Indians sing at social occasions such as dances. These are performed primarily for pleasure. A popular contemporary form of Indian social song called "49 Songs" is sung today by young people at gatherings known as powwows. Although there are many stories about the origin of the term "49 Songs," the one widespread in Oklahoma, where the songs reportedly originated, describes them as an Indian imitation of the songs and dances performed in the early 20th century at an Oklahoma carnival sideshow, "Days of 49" or "Girls of 49," which featured the decor of the California gold rush. Depending on the version, Indian youths were either too poor to attend or denied admission to the sideshow, so they set up their own "49" dances.

As these examples demonstrate, both ceremonial and nonceremonial songs are an integral part of Indian life. The significance of song to all Indians is expressed by these words of Netsilik Inuit Orpingalik: "It is as important to me to sing as to draw breath."▲

A buffalo hide painted with images of prominent figures in the narratives of the Kiowa Indians. In the center is Saynday, the supernatural being in human form who the Kiowa believe created the world.

TELLING STORIES

There is not a lake or mountain that has not connected with it some story of delight or wonder, and nearly every beast and bird is the subject of the story-teller, being said to have transformed itself at some prior time into some mysterious formation—of men going to live in the stars, and of imaginary beings in the air, whose rushing passage roars in the distant whirlwinds.

These words, in which Ojibwa author George Copway eloquently describes the importance of storytelling to him and his people, speak of the crucial role narratives play in all Indian cultures for both adults and children. Storytelling is one of the most important means a tribe has of educating its members in tribal beliefs and history. By listening to traditional stories, Indian peoples learn about the world and their place in it.

Often, the audiences for these narratives are children. In order to capture young people's attention, the stories are entertaining as well as instructive. According to Copway, "Some of these stories are most exciting, and so intensely interesting, that I have seen children during their relation, whose tears would flow most plentifully, and their breasts heave with thoughts too big for utterance."

Copway's experience is corroborated by Virginia Beavert, a Yakima Indian who collected her tribe's legends in *The Way It Was* (1974). In this book, the author points out that the legends were traditionally told by Yakima elders to their grandchildren during the winter while they and the children sat in a warm house filled with food. It was essential that each child listen attentively to learn the lessons the stories taught:

There were times when there was more than one story-teller involved, which made it a more interesting evening. Many questions were answered in the minds of the children; for instance why did the characters in the legend do things five times? It was explained that this was part of our lives, the parts of our bodies, the part of the religion, and many other things we take for granted in our everyday living.

Tribal groups categorize their narratives in various ways. Stories are sometimes divided into the true and the fictional, the sacred and the nonsacred, or some combination of these categories. The Winnebago, for instance, divide their narratives into *waikan* (what is sacred) and *worak* (what is recounted). Their sacred stories, which can only be told when snakes are in hibernation, tell of a past that is irretrievably lost and of a realm that is no longer attainable by man or spirits. Such stories have divine heroes and never end tragically. The recounted stories deal with the present and can be told at any time. The heroes of these stories are usually human beings, but in some rare cases are divine beings who have come to live with man. The Zuni divide their narratives into *chimikyánakowa* (origin stories), which may be told in any season and at any time of day, and *telapnaawe* (tales), which may be told only during the winter at night. Both types of narratives are set

in the long-ago past before contact with non-Indians.

Generally, scholars divide Indian narrative into myths and tales. Myths are ostensibly true stories of the prehistoric past. Tales may be true or fictional and are usually set in the historical period. Over the years, stories or portions of stories originally categorized as true myths can come to be thought of as fictional, and vice versa.

Indian myths usually describe a primal world peopled by animal spirits in human form, monsters, and aberrations. In the literatures of many tribes, after this period—the Myth Age—comes the Age of Transformation, during which the world takes its present form, animal people turn into animals, and other beings are transformed into natural landmarks. Following this era is the Historical Age, which includes all events that have occurred within human memory.

The general characteristics of American Indian oral narratives differ from those of Europeans and Americans and the written literature of non-Indians. Usually in Indian oral stories, plots are compressed and episodic, settings are simple, and style is terse. The characters are one-dimensional, rarely expressing thought or emotion. The stories dwell on characters' behavior only as much as it is necessary to advance the action. They also often contain inconsistencies of time, logic, and detail that are simply accepted by the listeners. Humor is another central element of American Indian narratives.

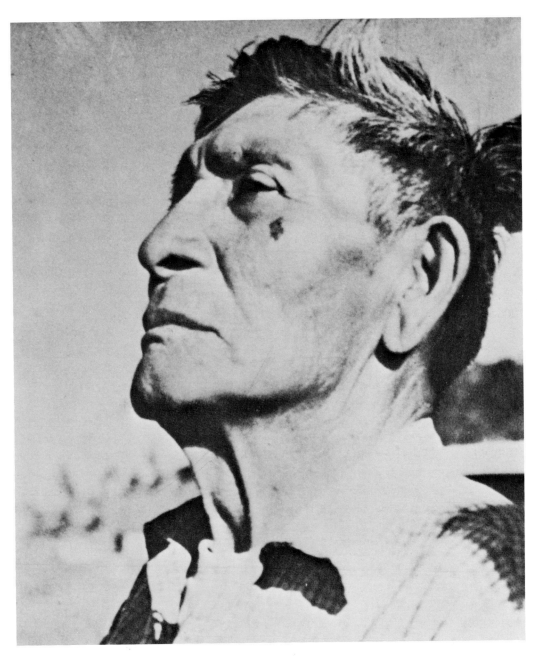

John Stands in Timber, author of Cheyenne Memories. *Like many other Indian autobiographers, Stands in Timber writes of the crucial role storytelling played in his education when he was a boy.*

However, its subtlety is sometimes lost in the stories' translation into English. Frank references to sexual acts and bodily functions are also common and are not considered distasteful by the stories' audiences.

Specific customs often accompany the act of storytelling. John Stands in Timber describes in *Cheyenne Memories* (1967) the rituals a tribal elder performed before he told a story:

An old storyteller would smooth the ground in front of him and make two marks in it with his right thumb, two with his left, and a double mark with both thumbs together. Then he would rub his hands, pass his right hand up his right leg to his waist, and touch his left hand and pass it on up his right arm to his breast. He did the same thing with his left and right hands going up the other side. Then he touched the marks on the ground with both hands, rubbed his hands together, and passed them over his head and all over his body.

In many Indian cultures, proper etiquette requires the audience to give the storyteller a gift of tobacco. Among the Ojibwa, stories about the Myth Age could only be told after the storyteller received a gift from the audience. The performance was followed by a feast. Ojibwa storytellers never told the title of the story until the story was finished.

Only those who observed the proper form and ceremony were permitted to hear the Cherokee's sacred myths. Boys who wanted to learn the sacred traditions of the tribe met with a tribal priest in a sweat lodge, a struc-ture filled with steam produced by pouring water over hot stones. There they sat up all night talking while their sweating removed the impurities from their bodies. At daybreak, the group traveled to a stream. The boys stripped their clothing, and then their teacher scratched their skin with a bone-tooth comb. The boys then waded in the water, faced the rising sun, and dipped themselves into the stream seven times while the priest recited prayers on the bank. As a special privilege, a boy who had completed this ceremony might be permitted to join the priests or myth keepers in the sleeping house, where they recited their rituals and myths as well as discussed their sacred knowledge.

In many tribes, storytellers use a special phrase or word to open or close stories or to elicit audience response. Seneca storytellers introduce origin stories with the words *Neh nih Che yonh en ja se* (When the world was new). The Pima and Papago begin fictional stories with phrases such as *sh hab wa chu'i na'ana* (They say it happened long ago) or *heki huh* (Long ago). They close their stories with *am o wa'i hug* (That is the end) or *am o wa'i at hoabdag* (That's the center of the basket). The latter phrase indicates that all the details of the story have been woven together. The Zuni begin their fictional narratives with *so'nachi*, which may mean "Now we are taking it up." The audience replies with *esso* (Yes, indeed), a word that is only used in storytelling. The narrator then says *sonti ino—te*, which may mean

This illustration by Al Momaday depicts the Kiowa's story of the origin of the Big Dipper. According to the legend, seven sisters were playing with their brother when suddenly he turned into a bear. Terrified, the girls climbed to the top of a giant tree trunk and were then borne into the sky, where they became the constellation's stars.

"Now it begins to be made." The audience responds with a second *esso*. The Yakima use a similar audience-response formula. The storyteller gains the children's attention by saying *Awacha nay!* (This is the way it was). The children respond with a loud *Ii* (Yes).

Because myths take place in the distant past, Indians sometime use archaic language when telling them. When a Zuni repeats tales that take place long ago, he avoids any modern words or phrases as well.

The Nez Percé also use specialized terms and language in some of their stories. Some animal characters have two names: the one by which the animal is ordinarily known and the one that designates its role in the myths. For instance, in Nez Percé myths, Coyote is called by a different name when he is presented as a trickster. Some animal characters also have distinctive speech characteristics. Fox speaks with utmost clarity and directness, Bear slurs consonants, and Skunk has a high-pitched, nasal voice.

Some tribal stories follow a specific structure. For example, Pima and Papago legends consist of an introduction, one or more episodes, and a conclusion. The introduction presents a setting, in which the characters are living in harmony. In each episode, this harmony is disrupted, leading the characters to take measures to reestablish it. The conclusion describes harmony's restoration.

Although American Indian oral narratives differ considerably in content, there are some common themes. One of the most prevalent is the creation of the world. The most complex creation stories are those by the Indians of the Southwest. One type told by tribes in Arizona, New Mexico, and southern California tells of the world's parents—the Sky Father and Earth Mother. Another type, of which the following Papago story is an example, describes the miraculous birth of a mythic hero who later creates the universe.

Long ago, they say, when the earth was not yet finished, darkness lay upon the water and they rubbed each other. The sound they made was like the sound at the edges of a pond.

There, on the water, in the darkness, in the noise, and in a very strong wind, a child was born. The child lay upon the water and did as a child does when it is being made to stop crying. (Like when its mother sings and tosses it up and down and walks back and forth with it). The wind always blew and carried the child everywhere. Whatever made the child took care of him, fed him, and raised him.

As the story continues, the infant, First Born, sends termites to gather algae. He then decides to make the algae into a seat solid enough so that the wind cannot blow it away. Sitting down to think about creating the earth, he sings:

Earth Medicine Man finished the earth.
Come near and see it and do something
    to it.
He made it round.
Come near and see it and do something
    to it.

By thinking and by singing his creation song, First Born finished the earth and then made all animal and plant life.

A third type of origin story describes the ascent of humans and other beings to the surface of the earth from a realm below. In the course of the ascent, the tribe's ways of life are established. In many such myths, emergence from a series of underworlds is followed by a migration, during which the tribe wanders from location to location; eventually, it reaches a special place where it settles.

In one version of the Zuni emergence myth, Awonawilona, an androgynous (both male and female) figure, creates the universe, which is filled with fog and has four levels, or rooms. Awonawilona then creates two priests (Ahayuuta), who descend to the fourth room, where they find human beings living in darkness. The Ahayuuta then lead the people, who pray to Awonawilona in the proper way, through the four rooms to the earth's surface. According to other versions of the myth, the people beneath the earth have an insectlike form. They and the priests who discover them are led from the underworld by a pair of twins. The elder twin orders the humans to make prayer sticks, symbols made of wood and feathers to which the Zuni pray. The sticks turn into trees or plants that the people use to climb from one room to the next. When the people finally emerge, they are dazzled by the sun.

Movement from a sky world to a water world characterizes the genesis stories of the Iroquoian tribes of the northeastern woodlands. According to the Seneca version recorded by Jesse Cornplanter, humankind originally existed in a celestial world, lit only by the white blossoms of a great tree. There, Chief's wife becomes pregnant from inhaling her husband's breath without his knowledge. The jealous chief then has

Raising the Slain Hero *by Jesse Cornplanter, who recorded many of the traditional narratives of Seneca Indians in* Legends of the Longhouse.

a dream that calls for the Tree of Light to be uprooted. He has this done, which creates an opening in the sky through which the sun shines. The chief persuades his unsuspecting wife to look down the hole and pushes her through it. In his anger, he also throws down plants and animals. As Chief's wife, Sky-woman, is falling, the water animals dive into the sea and gather some earth from its floor. They place the mud on the shell of Turtle. Landing on this soft earth, Sky-woman survives her fall. The mound then grows in size until it becomes the earth.

This example of a "fortunate fall" creation myth is closely related to another type of origin story—the earth-diver myth. Earth-diver myths are the most common genesis stories in North America and are especially predominant among the Algonquian-speaking tribes of the Great Lakes area. Such stories hold that a flood occurred after the creation of the universe and resulted in the re-creation of the present world from mud brought up from under the water by an animal referred to as earth-diver. Most often, the earth-diver is a muskrat.

A second type of American Indian narrative comprises stories about tribal culture heroes. A tribe's culture hero is a mythical character who creates the world as we know it, provides the resources and rituals humans need to survive, and defeats the enemies of humankind. A culture hero also possesses the power to shape various aspects of nature into their final form and to transform inanimate beings into animals and humans. He is usually of divine birth, frequently with Sun, Wind, or Stone as his father and a human as his mother. Often his mother dies or is killed before or during his birth.

In the legends of many tribes along the Pacific Coast, a culture hero shapes the world by stealing sun, fire, or water. Such myths are concerned not with the original owners of these things, but only with the culture hero's acquisition of them. An example is the Tsimshian story of how Raven brought light into a dark world. Before his birth, Raven's mother is unfaithful to her husband, a chief. In retaliation, the chief kills and buries her. Born after her burial, Raven is found and raised by another chief. After making himself a blanket of bird skins, Raven flies up to the sky, where he marries Sun's daughter. She bears a son, who accidentally falls down from the heavens and is found by an old

chief, who takes him home. At first, the boy will not eat, but when given a special food, he becomes so voracious that he eats all of the winter provisions of the chief's tribe.

Cast out for his selfish gluttony, the child assumes raven form and flies across the earth looking for food. On his flight, he sees some fishermen catching fish in the dark, for at that time the sun did not shine in the world. After the fishermen refuse his request for food, he threatens to make the sun shine.

To make good on his revenge, Raven flies to the home of the chief who owns daylight. Raven then transforms himself into a hemlock spike, which the chief's daughter swallows. She subsequently gives birth to Raven in baby form. The old chief so loves his new grandson that he allows him to play with a box containing sunlight. As soon as he gets the box, the grandchild transforms himself back into Raven, flies to the spot where the men are fishing, and opens the box to free the sun. Raven then sees that the fishermen are actually ghosts. While they speed away from the sunlight and from Raven, he devours their fish. To quench his thirst after eating so much, Raven steals fresh water from the old chief who possesses it. Discovering the theft, the chief pursues Raven, who in the chase accidentally spills the water. It then spreads all over the world.

According to a myth of the Shasta Indians, fire is stolen by their culture hero, Coyote, on a visit to the House of

Stone Giant Emerging, *a soapstone sculpture by contemporary Cayuga artist Joseph Jacobs.*
The stone giants of Iroquois tales were the most feared of the evil monsters of ancient times.

Pain, where fire lives. At the house, he finds young Pains who have been left there alone by their elders. The children suspect that he is Coyote, but he vehemently denies this. Coyote unfolds a long blanket, stretching it into the flames to make it catch fire. He then runs away and passes the fire to various birds to carry away while the elder Pains try vainly to catch them. Finally, Quail gives the fire to Turtle, who puts it under his armpit and jumps into the water. The Pains shoot him in the rear, creating a wound that becomes Turtle's tail, and then go away. Coyote is furious when he learns that Turtle dove under water with the fire. However, the fire is still burning, and Turtle throws it all around so that everybody can get some.

As these stories indicate, a culture hero is often a sly trickster who feels superior to all others and relies on cunning deceptions and mean tricks to achieve his goals. Because such trickster figures' appetites are enormous, incessant, and unrestrained by tribal taboos, myths about their mischievous acts provide outlets for socially unacceptable feelings and impulses and teach the consequences of improper behavior. Culture hero–tricksters can take many forms, but most often they are animals: Coyote in the Southwest, Raven in the Northwest and Arctic, Hare in the Great Lakes and Southeast, and Wolverine and Jay in Canada. Although tricksters are usually male, in some cultures, such as that of the Hopi, these characters are sometimes female.

Among the many trickster narratives are "hoodwinked duck" stories, which are widespread in the Midwest and Great Plains. In the Winnebago version, a hungry trickster persuades several naive ducks to keep their eyes closed and dance while he sings. An accomplished con artist, the trickster warns the ducks that their eyes will become red if they open them. While the obedient ducks dance happily with closed eyes, the trickster quickly devours them until one duck opens his eyes and alerts the others. Most of the remaining ducks escape.

But a trickster's plans do not always succeed. Often he gets his comeuppance after a temporary victory. In a Sioux story, Iktomi (Spider) decides that he wants to be a medicine man after watching some men pray in the high mountains for four days and nights without food. Iktomi prepares himself properly by singing sacred songs in a sweatlodge and swabbing his body with sage. But all the time, he is thinking, "These Indians, these medicine men don't pray. They just go on the hill, sit around and look around." When he emerges from the sweatlodge, Iktomi goes up into the mountains, where he sits without praying for four days. Finally, a herd of buffalo comes running toward him. In terror, he hides in some bushes and desperately begins to pray, "O Great Spirit, help me. These buffalo are going to kill me." The Great Spirit takes pity on Iktomi and turns the buffalo away. When Iktomi returns to his camp, he vows, "I'll never be a med-

continued on page 57

PAINTING TRADITION

For centuries, Indians have used oral and written literatures to express their worldview. Paintings also have long been used by Native Americans to communicate their ideas about the universe, nature, and humanity.

Like Indian literatures, Indian painting has changed through time. For instance, throughout the 19th century, Native American artisans gradually abandoned natural vegetable pigments in favor of commercially manufactured watercolors and oils because these paints were easier to use and could produce more vivid colors. Many Indian painters also adopted pictorial styles associated with American and European art, often doing so in order to help make their work more marketable to non-Indians.

Despite these changes, contemporary Indian painters have not rejected their roots. Some artists pay homage to the past by using certain conventions of earlier Indian art. They often choose, for example, to imitate the simple lines and flat colors of the figures traditionally found in Indian hide paintings and pottery decoration.

Native American painters also celebrate their heritage through the content of their art. A major source of inspiration are ancient Indian narratives, particularly the myths of the origin of the world and the stories of the adventures of tribal culture heroes. Just as many of today's Indian writers employ Western literary forms—such as the novel and the poem—to explain their tribal traditions and histories, these painters use their art to tell old stories in a new way to a new audience.

A detail from The Legend of the Snake Clan, *a hide painting by 20th-century Hopi artist Fred Kabotie.*

The Iroquois story of creation is depicted in this 1980 painting entitled *Creations Battle* by Mohawk artist John Fadden. The conflict between good and evil in the universe is represented by the struggle between Sky Woman's sons, The Good Twin and The Evil Twin. The Good Twin created all the good in the universe, including plants, animals, rivers, and streams. To counteract his brother's work, The Evil Twin produced poisonous plants, thorns, diseases, and monsters. However, The Evil Twin was not ultimately powerful enough to triumph in the creation battle. As a final stroke, The Good Twin created human beings to enjoy all the good he had made for them.

A Navajo creation myth is represented in the 1938 painting **Sun King and His Wife** by Gerald Nailor. Pictured is the Sun's visit with Changing Woman, who as a result gives birth to twin sons, Child Born of Water and Monster Slayer. During the twins' childhood, Changing Woman creates the Navajo people from a mixture of cornmeal and scrapings of her own skin.

Navajo artist Andy Tsinajinnie portrays his tribe's origin story in **The Fourth World** (1960). In the center of this painting are the three lower worlds through which the Navajo believe all creatures of the universe had to travel before they could reach the world they now inhabit. In each world, humans co-exist peacefully with other animals. Thus, the story illustrates the importance of maintaining harmony within a group, a value the Navajo cherish.

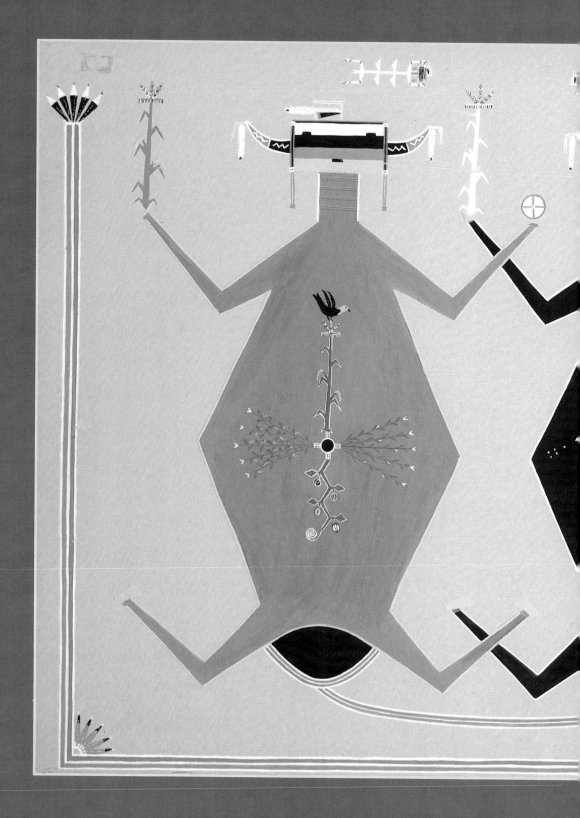

The divine creators of the first human couple are illustrated in **Mother Earth and Father Sky, Male Shootingway**, *a 1936 watercolor copy of a Navajo sand painting. According to Navajo and Pueblo narratives, the pair are the ancestors of the Hero Twins, who vanquished the forces of evil in order to make the world safe for humans to inhabit.*

Mother Earth is colored turquoise and holds a corn plant and a basket containing corn pollen. In the center of her body is the water that covered the earth when people had first journeyed from the underworld to the earth's surface. From the water's surface sprout four sacred plants brought up from below—corn, beans, squash, and tobacco.

Father Sky's body is black and covered with white markings representing the Milky Way, crescent moon, and constellations. He holds an ear of corn and a blue basket with corn pollen sprinkled in four directions.

The figures of Father Sky and Mother Earth have identical shapes, symbolizing cosmic harmony. They are also linked by the lines of sacred pollen between their mouths and between their reproductive organs. Both are wearing buffalo horns marked with lightning and identical headdresses of turkey and eagle feathers.

The character of Coyote appears in many tribes' traditional stories. Coyote is usually a clever trickster but is often outsmarted by the victims of his pranks. The traditional figure of the Coyote trickster has been revitalized through the work of Maidu artist Harry Fonseca. In his series of Coyote paintings, Fonseca blends old beliefs and stories with elements of modern art. Fonseca says, "I believe my Coyote paintings to be the most contemporary statement I have painted in regard to traditional belief and contemporary reality. I have taken a universal Indian image, Coyote, and have placed him in a contemporary setting." Fonseca has captured Coyote in many identities, painting the trickster as an actor, a rock star, and a tourist. This work, Koshare with Watermelon (1983), depicts two coyotes as Pueblo clowns.

Eskimo Hunter *(1959) by Kivetoruk Moses portrays the story of an Inuit hunter who is captured by a huge eagle. Attempting to escape, the Inuit wounds the eagle's leg with a knife. Listening to the heartbeat of the dying eagle, the hunter learns the rhythm that the Inuit play on the drum to accompany their ceremonial dancing.*

Saynday, a supernatural being who created the Kiowa people, is portrayed in Sharron Ahtone Harjo's 1972 work, **Saynday and the Prairie Dogs.** *In the story depicted, Saynday has tricked a group of prairie dogs into closing their eyes and then kills them one by one. He spares the one animal who is smart enough to keep her eyes open and chooses her to become the mother of all prairie dogs.*

Hopi artist Fred Kabotie's hide painting, **The Legend of the Snake Clan,** *depicts the story of Tiyo, the son of a village chief. Tiyo encounters a kiva (religious house) whose members are able to turn themselves into snakes by putting on snakeskin costumes. With the help of Spider Woman (a figure in Navajo mythology), Tiyo is able to overpower the snake people and is accepted into the clan. Tiyo marries one of the Snake Clan women. Their children become the founders of the Snake Clan at the village of Walpi.*

continued from page 48

icine man again because I haven't the power, I haven't the knowledge and the wisdom to do what they do. I'll just have to do something else." So once again Iktomi returns to his mischief making.

There are many other themes and motifs found in Indian myths. Some are concerned with lesser beings, often twins, who help the gods or humankind by slaying monsters. Others recount a person's attempts to bring his or her beloved back from the world of the dead. Still another genre, Star-husband stories, combine elements found in many creation and culture-hero myths. In these stories, an earth woman who yearns to marry a star ascends to the sky, where she becomes pregnant. While there, she breaks a tribal taboo. She subsequently descends to the earth, frequently by means of a rope she lowers from her sky home. She dies either when she lands or when giving birth to a son. Often, the second part of the story deals with the adventures of her Sky Son, who is adopted by an old woman and becomes a culture hero.

The tradition of storytelling remains strong among Indian peoples. They not only tell the old stories, but also create many new versions. Ancient narratives have also been kept alive in the written works of American Indian authors. Today, as yesterday, these stories entertain and teach each generation of Indians about their rich tribal heritage. ▲

Chief Joseph, whose eloquent pleas for justice made him one of the best-known Indian leaders in the late 19th century.

ORATORY
AND
AUTOBIOGRAPHY

Two genres of American Indian literatures historically bridge the gap between oral and written works: oratory and autobiography. Speeches were traditionally a part of the oral literature of many tribes. But after contact with non-Indians, Indian oratory began to be preserved in writing by white listeners. Full-length autobiographies were not part of the literary tradition of American Indians. The Indians did, however, incorporate autobiographical accounts into their oral traditions. Many Indian life histories were dictated to non-Indians, and others were written by the subjects themselves. Like later Indian oratory, these works were often created by their Indian authors to tell a white audience of their tribe and its heritage, as well as of their own personal experiences.

Oratory has long been a skill highly regarded by many Indian tribes. For instance, among the Plains Indians, public speaking and good citizenship were synonymous. Oratory was incorporated into most forms of public ceremony and was also an important means of settling political and legal disputes.

The Iroquois particularly emphasize oratory in their ceremonies. For instance, the Iroquois Ritual of Condolence contains addresses by priests to supernatural powers and to the community. When repeating traditional orations, Iroquois speakers may shorten them by reciting only the essential words or lengthen them by repeating statements. The excerpt on the following page from "The Creation," the opening speech of a thanksgiving ritual given by Enos Williams (Mohawk/Ca-

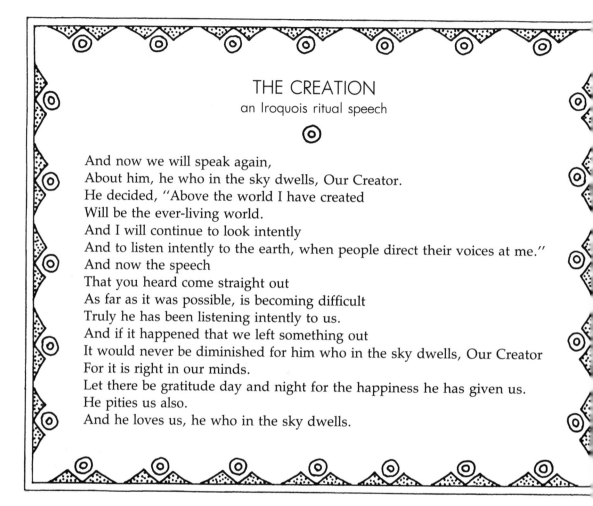

THE CREATION
an Iroquois ritual speech

And now we will speak again,
About him, he who in the sky dwells, Our Creator.
He decided, "Above the world I have created
Will be the ever-living world.
And I will continue to look intently
And to listen intently to the earth, when people direct their voices at me."
And now the speech
That you heard come straight out
As far as it was possible, is becoming difficult
Truly he has been listening intently to us.
And if it happened that we left something out
It would never be diminished for him who in the sky dwells, Our Creator
For it is right in our minds.
Let there be gratitude day and night for the happiness he has given us.
He pities us also.
And he loves us, he who in the sky dwells.

yuga) probably in 1970, illustrates Iroquois oratorical style.

Nonceremonial speeches can have many purposes. Some are a part of Indians' political life, such as addresses made at council meetings and formal petitions to the federal or state governments. Other forms of oratory were reserved for wartime. For instance, speeches were often made to inspire warriors or to celebrate a victory over an enemy.

Although Indian oratory is more commonly associated with formal speeches, informal, personal speeches often deeply moved their audiences. In the following example of informal oratory, dating from the late 19th century, a young Crow warrior named Doubleface describes how he regained his courage to battle his enemies after being filled with doubts:

I used to think that since my birth I had had many sorrows. It turns out that there was something in store for me. I was grieving, but I did not know that today all manner of sorrow would be coming to a head. The women at my home are miserable, I daresay. "How are the captive Crow faring?" they are thinking to themselves. My poor dear housemates, my distressed kin, the enemy makes them sit under the dripping water, he is ever abusing them, he thinks his men are the only ones to be brave. What can I do to distress him, I wonder?

You Above, if there be one who knows what is going on, repay me today for the distress I have suffered. Inside the Earth, if there be any one there who knows what is going on, repay me for the distress I have suffered. The One Who causes things, Whoever he be, I have now had my fill of life. Grant me death, my sorrows are overabundant. Though children are timid, they die harsh deaths, it is said. Though women are timid, you make them die harsh deaths. I do not want to live long; were I to live long, my sorrows would be overabundant. I do not want it!

Traditionally, most Indian orators were men. Plains Indians only occasionally allowed a female warrior or strong medicine woman to speak in public. But tribal members would not listen to even these women unless they were considered virtuous and chaste according to the standards of the tribe. Despite these restrictions, some women did become influential speakers. For instance, Paiute women contributed to the deliberations of their tribal council. In *Life Among the Piutes* (1883), Paiute author Sarah Winnemucca Hopkins comments that "women know as much as the men do, and their advice is often asked."

A major form of American Indian oratory that developed after Indians began to have contact with non-Indians was speeches made by Indian leaders at meetings with representatives of non-Indian governments. Because these speeches are frequently reprinted, they are perhaps the best-known works of Indian oratory. But it should be remembered that these works were usually written down by white members of the orator's audience, so the accounts are possibly not true to the content and form of the speech as it was originally performed.

The history of a speech delivered by Chief Seattle, leader of the Duwamish and Suquamish Indians, at the Point Elliott treaty negotiations of 1855 illustrates how inaccurately some Indian oratory has been recorded. Two short speeches are preserved among the documents of the negotiations, but neither bears any resemblance to the speech now commonly attributed to Chief Seattle in American and European publications. The first published version of this popular speech was presented to the public by Dr. H. A. Smith in 1887, more than 30 years after the chief is said to have delivered it. Possibly, Smith based his versions on notes made in his

An 1865 photograph of Chief Seattle, whose speech at the Point Elliot treaty negotiations of 1855 is one of the most famous works of Indian oratory. The version most often reprinted probably bears little resemblance to the speech the chief actually gave, however. The published account was most likely reconstructed by a white man from sketchy notes 30 years after he had heard Chief Seattle deliver the speech.

diary while Chief Seattle was speaking. This version was subsequently revised by others.

One of the first Indian speeches to be published was the following plea made by Wahunsonacock, also known as King Powhatan, to the colonists of Jamestown in 1609. The speech was written down by Captain John Smith.

Why should you take by force that from us which you can have by love? Why should you destroy us, who have provided you with food? What can you get by war? We can hide our provisions, and fly into the woods; and then you must consequently famish by wronging your friends. What is the cause of your jealousy? You see us unarmed, and willing to supply your wants, if you come in a friendly manner, and not with swords and guns as to invade an enemy.

Throughout the next two centuries, English and, later, American settlers wrestled control of most of the Indian lands in what is now the eastern United States. Aware that whites were not going to cease their conquest, the Shawnee chief Tecumseh attempted in the 1810s to persuade Indians living south of the Ohio River and west of the Appalachian Mountains to unite in a confederation to oppose the invaders. In 1811, Tecumseh made the following speech emphasizing why Indians must continue their fight against white encroachment:

Where today are the Pequot? Where are the Narragansett, the Mohican, the Pocanet, and other powerful tribes of our people? They have vanished before the avarice and oppression of the white man, as snow before the summer sun. . . . Will we let ourselves be destroyed in our turn, without making an effort worthy of our race? Shall we, without a struggle, give up our homes, our lands, bequeathed to us by the Great Spirit? The graves of our dead and everything that is dear and sacred to us? . . . I know you will say with me, Never! Never!

Indians' love of the land and commitment to family is eloquently expressed in the excerpt below from a speech delivered by Chief Joseph of the Nez Percé in 1879 to congressmen and officials in Washington, D.C. Unfortunately, Chief Joseph's attempt to persuade the government to allow his people to return to tribal lands was unsuccessful:

. . . In order to have all people understand how much land we owned, my father planted poles all around it and said:

"Inside is the home of my people—the white man may take the land outside. Inside this boundary all our people were born. It circles around the graves of our fathers, and we will never give up these graves to any man." . . . My father sent for me. I saw he was dying. I took his hand in mine. He said: "My son, my body is returning to my mother earth, and my spirit is going very soon to see the Great Spirit Chief. When I am gone, think of your country. You are chief of these people. They look to you to guide them. Always remember that your father never sold his country. You must stop your ears whenever you are asked to sign a treaty selling your home. A few years more, and white men will be all around you. They have their eyes on this land. My son, never forget my dying words. This country holds your father's body. Never sell the bones of your father and mother." I pressed my father's hand and told him I would protect his grave with my life. My father smiled and passed away to the spirit-land.

I buried him in that beautiful valley of winding waters. I love that land more than all the rest of the world. A man who would not love his father's grave is worse than a wild animal.

Although Indian nations and the United States no longer negotiate treaties, American Indian oratory is a continuing tradition. Today, Indian speakers are equally likely to be heard during the performance of an ancient ceremony as during a congressional hearing dealing with the legal rights of Indians.

Indian life histories achieved considerable popularity during the 19th and early 20th centuries. Like the narratives of African American slaves published during this period, they were of particular interest to whites who were critical of U.S. government policies that resulted in the mistreatment of other peoples living within America's borders. Many of these readers thought of Indians as "vanishing Americans" and were eager to learn of Indian cultures that seemed to be disappearing in the face of white settlement of the western frontier.

The first autobiography to be published was *A Son of the Forest* (1829) by William Apes (Pequot, b. 1798). Apes spent most of his childhood as an indentured servant to several white families. He later converted to Methodism, ran away to join the army during the War of 1812, and became an ordained minister in 1829. Apes's book was strongly influenced by non-Indians' published spiritual confessions, a popular genre of the period. Like these works, his autobiography describes his perilous journey to salvation, fall from grace, and subsequent rededication to Christianity. But, unusual for the time, Apes's book is strongly critical of

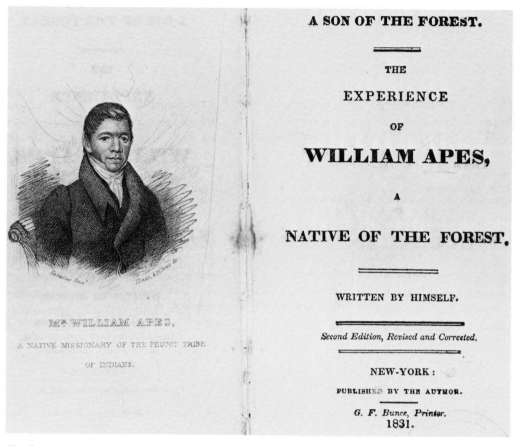

A SON OF THE FOREST.

THE

EXPERIENCE

OF

WILLIAM APES,

A

NATIVE OF THE FOREST.

WRITTEN BY HIMSELF.

Second Edition, Revised and Corrected.

NEW-YORK:
PUBLISHED BY THE AUTHOR.

G. F. Bunce, Printer.
1831.

Mr WILLIAM APES,

A NATIVE MISSIONARY OF THE PEQUOT TRIBE

OF INDIANS.

The frontispiece and title page of the second edition of William Apes's Son of the Forest, *the first published autobiography written by an American Indian.*

whites' treatment of Indians. Apes was particularly angered that the whites with whom he lived as a child had taught him to be terrified of his own people and often threatened to punish him by sending him into the forest to live among them.

. . . the great fear I entertained of my brethren, was occasioned by the many stories I had heard of their cruelty towards the whites—how they were in the habit of killing and scalping men, women and children. But the whites did not tell me that they were in a great majority of instances the aggressors—that they had imbrued their hands in the life blood of my brethren, driven them from their once peaceful and happy homes—that they introduced among them the fatal and exterminating diseases of civilized life. If the whites had told me how cruel they had been to the poor Indian, I should have apprehended as much harm from them.

Another important early Indian autobiography is *Life, History, and Travels of Kah-ge-ga-gah-bowh* (1847) by George Copway (Ojibwa, 1818–69). Copway was born near the mouth of the Trent River in Upper Canada and lived as a traditional Ojibwa until he was converted to Methodism when he was nine years old. After his marriage to Elizabeth Howell, a white woman, Copway served as a missionary in Wisconsin, Minnesota, and Ontario, Canada. Returning to the United States, Copway was befriended by American Methodists who encouraged him to launch a new career as a lecturer and writer on Indian affairs. Like *A Son of the Forest*, Copway's autobiography reflects the tradition of spiritual confessions. Although the book includes information about Ojibwa traditions, it emphasizes Copway's commitment to Christianity and his belief that education is the best method of converting Indians. Copway characterizes himself as a "noble savage," a common 19th-century Indian stereotype. But Copway's tender portrayals of Indian family life in the book contradict the images of Indian savagery that were often found in the popular press of his day. Copway's book was well received by whites; in one year, it was reprinted six times. The volume's blend of myth, history, and personal experience also established a structure used by many later Indian autobiographers.

One of the few Indian life histories published in the next three decades was *Life Among the Piutes* by Sarah Winne-

Sarah Winnemucca Hopkins, author of Life Among the Piutes. *In this autobiography, Hopkins describes the Paiute's struggles with whites and the role of women in Paiute society.*

mucca Hopkins, the only Indian woman to publish a full-length personal history in the late 19th century. Born near the the Humboldt River in Nevada, Hopkins was the granddaughter of Truckee, who she claimed was chief of all the Paiutes, and the daughter of Old Winnemucca, who succeeded his father as chief. Because Hopkins and her family followed Truckee's policy of trying to peacefully coexist with whites, she spent much of her life serving as a liaison between the Paiute and white settlers and government officials.

Hopkins grew disillusioned with federal Indian policy, moving her to take the Paiute cause to the public. Encouraged by the success of her first lecture in San Francisco in 1879, she toured the East, delivering more than 300 speeches. She reached an even larger audience with the publication of *Life Among the Piutes*, one of the most imaginative personal and tribal histories of the period. With a sharp eye for detail, Hopkins recreates scenes and dialogues that give her book a sense of immediacy missing from many other histories of the period. Particularly interesting are her portrayals of her childhood terror of the whites her grandfather so respected and of her role as a liaison between Indians and whites during the Bannock War. Hopkins also discusses the status of women in Paiute society, constantly reminding her white readers that Paiute women had more opportunity to influence their councils than white women had with their governments. Although Hopkins praises

white achievements, she eloquently attacks the religious hypocrisy of white Christians determined to take all Indian land and exterminate its inhabitants:

Your carbines rise upon the bleak shore, and your so-called civilization sweeps inland from the ocean wave; but, oh, my God! leaving its pathway marked by crimson lines of blood, and strewed by the bones of two races, the inheritor and the invader; and I am crying out to you for justice.

In the 1890s and early 1900s, many western Indians began writing autobiographies. The most influential and widely read were those by Charles Eastman (a.k.a. Ohiyesa, Sioux, 1858–1939), one of the first Indians to earn a medical degree. Until he was 15, Eastman led the life of a traditional Santee Sioux boy, isolated from contact with whites. This free life ended when his father enrolled him in school in Flandreau, Dakota Territory. Eastman later attended Dartmouth College and Boston University Medical School, from which he received his M.D. in 1890. Eastman became a physician at the Pine Ridge Indian Reservation in South Dakota, where he met and married Elaine Goodale, a Massachusetts writer and teacher. Although her name appears on only two of Eastman's books, she collaborated with him on all his works.

Eastman's first autobiographical work, *Indian Boyhood* (1902), describes his life until age 15. The opening lines express the spirit Eastman hoped to transmit to his readers: "What boy

An illustration by Herman Morton Stoops from Luther Standing Bear's Stories of the Sioux *(1934). Stoops based his drawings on notes supplied in sketch form by an Oglala Sioux named Yellow Bird.*

would not be an Indian for a while when he thinks of the freest life in the world? This life was mine. Everyday there was a real hunt. There was real game." Eastman's second autobiography, *From the Deep Woods to Civilization* (1916), tells of his experiences as an adult in the white world. It also reveals his deepening sense of his own Indianness and questions the value of white ways. Eastman strongly criticizes the U.S. government, particularly its indifference to the hunger and misery of Sioux Indians living on reservations. In all his works, Eastman attempted to re-

veal to his white audience the world-views, customs, literature, and history of the Indians so that non-Indian Americans might appreciate and emulate Indian virtues.

Eastman's autobiographies inspired other Sioux writers, such as Luther Standing Bear and Zitkala-Ša, to write their own personal narratives. Like Eastman, Standing Bear (a.k.a. Ota K'te, ca. 1868–1939) belonged to the generation of Sioux who witnessed the end of their traditional life with their settlement on reservations. He was among the first class at the Carlisle Indian School, established in Pennsylvania in 1879 by Richard Henry Pratt, an army officer, to educate and "civilize" young Indians. Standing Bear eventually joined Buffalo Bill's Wild West Show, which toured the United States and England in 1902. By 1912, he had settled in California, where he became a movie actor, lecturer, and volunteer for Indian causes. Late in life, he began a career as an author when he wrote *My People, the Sioux* (1928), assisted by E. A. Brininstool, a book that includes vignettes of Sioux life. Especially moving are his descriptions of his journey to Carlisle and subsequent life there. In 1933, he published *Land of the Spotted Eagle*, which he wrote with the assistance of Melvin Gilmore and Warcaziwin (also spelled Wahcaziwin). This volume focuses on Sioux beliefs and customs and is highly critical of whites' treatment of Indians. Standing Bear also wrote *My Indian Boyhood* (1931), a children's book.

Anthropologist and author Francis La Flesche, 1902.

Zitkala-Ša (a.k.a. Gertrude Bonnin, 1876–1938) in 1900 and 1901 published autobiographical essays in the *Atlantic Monthly* that were subsequently reprinted in *American Indian Stories* (1921). These essays tell of Zitkala-Ša's girlhood and recount traditional Sioux stories. Throughout her life, Zitkala-Ša was very active in Indian rights organizations.

Another Plains Indian who wrote a fine autobiography is Francis La Flesche (Omaha, 1857–1932). Trained as a linguist, La Flesche was one of the first Indians to become an anthropologist. *The Middle Five* (1900) describes his life as a student in a Presbyterian mission school in northeastern Nebraska during the Civil War. He creates lively and amusing portraits of the boys at the school, their activities, and their interactions with their parents and school authorities as they learn to adjust to a new culture.

The great age of narrated autobiographies came in the first half of the 20th century, when anthropologists who recognized the importance of the life history as a means of understanding tribal cultures collected numerous personal narratives. The most popular of these narrated life histories today is *Black Elk Speaks* (1932), which was recorded by John G. Neihardt. The book tells of the life and visions of a Sioux medicine man. It also portrays his tribe's worldviews and customs both before and after the Sioux were forced onto reservations and contains accounts of the Battle of Little Bighorn told by Black Elk and others who witnessed the event or heard stories from eyewitnesses. Far more literary than most Indian autobiographies, *Black Elk Speaks* expresses Black Elk's story in Neihardt's tone and style.

Another interesting narrated life history is *Lame Deer, Seeker of Visions* (1972) by John Fire (Lame Deer, b. 1900) and Richard Erdoes. It gives a humorous account of a Sioux who was part holy man and part scamp living after the beginning of the reservation period.

An additional type of Indian life history is that recorded in writing by the subjects and later edited by scholars. Among the most interesting works of this genre is *The Warrior Who Killed Custer*, which was originally written in the Dakota language by Chief White Bull (Sioux, b. 1850).

Another example is *Mourning Dove: A Salish Autobiography* (1990), which was edited by Jay Miller. Miller constructed the volume from various drafts and fragments prepared by Mourning Dove (a.k.a. Christine Quintasket, Colville, 1888–1936), who died before she could complete the manuscript. Using her own life as an example, Mourning Dove devotes several chapters to the role of women in American Indian society.

The best-known Indian autobiographies of the late 20th century are those written by N. Scott Momaday (Kiowa, b. 1934). Although born in Lawton, Oklahoma, Momaday spent much of his youth in the Southwest on Navajo, San Carlos Apache, and Jemez reservations in New Mexico and Arizona, where his Kiowa father and part-Cherokee mother worked. One of the first American Indians to receive a Ph.D. in English, Momaday is now a distinguished professor at the University of Arizona.

Momaday's *Way to Rainy Mountain* (1969) chronicles the Kiowa's origin and migration to Oklahoma, their life both before and after the reservation period, and his own quest for his tribal roots. In this highly imaginative, poetic work, Momaday incorporates Kiowa myths, tribal and family history, and personal reminiscences. An introductory essay, prologue, epilogue, and two poems frame three chapters that describe the emergence, ascendance, and decline of the Kiowa culture. The book pays tribute to memory—tribal, familial, and personal—and emphasizes the inevitability of change and loss.

Momaday's *Names* (1976) is a more conventional autobiography. It is a fascinating account of both sides of his family as well as a detailed and poignant description of his boyhood. In this volume, Momaday argues that individuals are molded by the particular location they inhabit.

Another widely published American Indian author who has written an autobiography is Gerald Vizenor (Ojibwa, b. 1934). He received his B.A. from the University of Minnesota and in the mid-1950s served in the U.S. Army in Japan. After becoming a journalist, Vizenor wrote for the *Minneapolis Tribune* and served as a contributing ed-

In The Way to Rainy Mountain *(1969), N. Scott Momaday recounts the Kiowa's history and his own search for tribal roots. This illustration by Al Momaday (the author's father) from the book depicts a meteor shower that occurred in 1833, one of the earliest events recorded in the tribe's calendars.*

itor to the *Twin Citian*. Currently, he is professor of English, David Burr Chair of Letters, at the University of Oklahoma. His *Interior Landscapes* (1990) is by turns poignant, sprightly, and satiric; in it Vizenor records the history of his ancestors on the White Earth Reservation, recounts the unsolved murder of his father that occurred when the author was a toddler, and describes his own evolution as a writer. Vizenor vividly re-creates his childhood spent living in poverty with his mother, relatives, or foster parents; his uneasy relationship with his mother; and his eventual love of his stern stepfather, whom his mother abandoned and who died shortly thereafter in an accident at work. In the third grade, Vizenor began to escape into an imaginary world he created, where he had a made-up trickster friend named Erdupps Mac-Churbbs. The author also describes his experiences in the army and in various social service, journalistic, and academic jobs.

American Indian life histories and autobiographies constitute one of the largest genres of these peoples' literatures. For almost 200 years, the accounts of their lives that American Indians narrated to others or wrote themselves have been an invaluable source of information about them and their cultures. ▲

Ridley & Blood Sc.

Rev. Samson Occom.

Indian Preacher.

Pub by Williams & Smith Stationers Court 10 d.r 1808.

An 1808 portrait of Samson Occom, a Mohegan Indian who served as a Methodist missionary. Occom's Sermon Preached at the Execution of Moses Paul, an Indian (1772) was the first published work in English by an Indian author.

WRITING
IN
ENGLISH:
1772–1967

By the late 18th century, Indian authors began not only to write in English but also to use literary forms developed by Europeans. These forms included sermons, protest literature, tribal histories, and travel accounts. Like the Indian autobiographers, writers in these genres hoped that their prose would make their white audiences recognize Indians' humanity and the significance of their tribal cultures and history. The emphasis of their writings consequently changed over time, always paralleling political developments and the U.S. government's ever-changing Indian policy.

The first Indian author to publish in English was Samson Occom (Mohegan, 1723–92), a Methodist missionary renowned for his powerful preaching. Occom was the pupil of the Reverend Eleazar Wheelock, who sent his Indian student to England from 1765 to 1768.

While there, Occom raised money for the Indian Charity School, an institution Wheelock founded in Hanover, New Hampshire, which later became Dartmouth College. Occom's major work was a sermon he preached at the execution of Moses Paul, a Mohegan Indian convicted of committing a murder while he was intoxicated. The sermon combines a deep concern for the effects of alcohol on Indian life with the traditions of non-Indian clergymen's execution sermons, which were then popular in the United States. Occom's work was published in 1772 and was so well received that it was subsequently reprinted at least 19 times.

One of the most forceful Indian writers of the early 19th century was William Apes (Pequot, b. 1798). His *Indian Nullification of the Unconstitutional Laws of Massachusetts, Relative to the Marshpee Tribe* (1835) is a well-documented account of the grievances of this tribe, which Apes joined and encouraged in its fight for justice. Apes's final work is the eloquent *Eulogy on King Philip* (1836), which protests England's mistreatment of Indians in the 17th and 18th centuries. Apes claimed that he was a descendant of King Philip, a Wampanoag leader who instigated an Indian rebellion in New England in the 1670s.

Many 19th-century American Indian authors wrote histories of their tribes based on oral traditions. The first such history to be published was *Sketches of Ancient History of the Six Nations* (probably 1827) by David Cusick (Tuscarora, died c. 1840). Other Indian authors soon began to follow Cusick's example by writing of the traditions and cultures of their tribes. Many of these histories were created as a response to U.S. government policy. In the early 19th century, the federal government applied increasing pressure on Indians living east of the Mississippi River to relocate, or remove, to lands farther west so that whites could settle the Indians' homelands. Authors of tribal histories hoped that their works would remind whites of their tribes' long existence as peoples and convince them to respect the Indians' rights to the land they traditionally occupied.

George Copway (Ojibwa, 1818–69) published his *Traditional History and Characteristic Sketches of the Ojibway Nation* in 1850. In this work, Copway emphasizes the importance of oral tradition as a basis for Indian history. Peter Jones (Kahkewaquonaby, 1803–56), a Methodist missionary like Copway, wrote his own *History of the Ojibway [sic] Indians* in 1861. Jones's work is far more authoritative than Copway's, but the best and most complete history of the Ojibwa written in the 1800s is *History of the Ojibways, Based upon Traditions and Oral Statements* by Charles Warren (Ojibwa, 1825–53). Completed in 1852, the book was not published until 1885, more than 30 years after Warren's death. Highly respected by Indians and non-Indians alike, Warren worked as an interpreter and served as a member of the Minnesota state legislature.

Other tribal histories written during this period include Peter Dooyentate Clarke's (Wyandot) *Origin and Traditional History of the Wyandotts [sic], and Sketches of Other Indian Tribes in North America* (1870); Chief Elias Johnson's (Tuscarora) *Legends, Traditions and Laws of the Iroquois, or Six Nations, and History of Tuscarora Indians* (1881); and Chief Andrew J. Blackbird's (a.k.a. Mackawdegbenessy, Ottawa, born c. 1827) *History of the Ottawa and Chippewa Indians of Michigan; A Grammar of Their Language, and Personal and Family History of the Author* (1887).

In the late 19th century, some Indians published accounts of their travels abroad. Maungwudaus (a.k.a. George Henry, Ojibwa, born c. 1810), a lapsed Methodist convert and cousin of Peter Jones, described his adventures with his traveling band of Indian performers in a pamphlet entitled *An Account of the Chippewa Indians, who have*

A Cherokee delegation of treaty negotiators, photographed in Washington, D.C., in 1866. On the far left is John Rollin Ridge, who in addition to being a renowned statesman was one of the few Indians in the 19th century to write both fiction and poetry.

been *Travelling among the Whites, in the United States, England, Ireland, Scotland, France and Belgium* (1848). Copway recounted his travels in *Running Sketches of Men and Places, in England, France, Germany, Belgium, and Scotland* (1851), the first full-length travel book by an Indian.

One of the few Indians to write fiction and poetry in the 19th century was John Rollin Ridge (1827–67). Ridge was

the half-Cherokee grandson of Major Ridge, one of the most influential leaders of the tribe before its removal from the southeastern United States to Indian Territory (now Oklahoma) in the late 1830s. Late in his teens, John Rollin Ridge shot a man—probably in self-defense—and fled in 1850 to the gold fields of California. Writing under the name Yellow Bird (a literal translation of his Cherokee name Cheesquatalawny), Ridge became a regular contributor to San Francisco periodicals. He later became the owner and editor of several California newspapers.

Ridge's *Life and Adventures of Joaquín Murieta* (1854) is the first novel written by an Indian author. It tells the story of a hardworking, ambitious man of Spanish and Indian ancestry who, echoing the experiences of the Cherokee, is driven off his land by greedy whites. Only after his brother is killed does Murieta devote his life to getting revenge against his oppressors. A good man driven to violent deeds by injustice, Murieta is a gallant gentleman to women, a courageous leader to his men, and an unrelenting enemy to his foes. This romance, reminiscent of the legend of Robin Hood, inspired later Mexican American writers and initiated a flood of stories about this character. As the following passage illustrates, the novel races at a breathless pace, filled with derring-do and punctuated by gunfire:

He dashed along that fearful trail as he had been mounted upon a spirit-steed, shouting as he passed:
"I am Joaquín! Kill me if you can!"
Shot after shot came clanging around his head, and bullet after bullet flattened on the wall of salt at his right. In the midst of the first firing, his hat was knocked from his head, and left his long black hair streaming behind him.

Ridge was also a poet. Most of his poetry was written before he was 20 but published posthumously (after the au-

An 1859 drawing of the title character of John Rollin Ridge's novel, The Life and Adventures of Joaquín Murieta *(1854).*

thor's death) in a collection titled *Poems* (1868). Although the majority reflect the sentimentality of most popular non-Indian American literature of the period, one poem, "Arkansas Root Doctor," reveals Ridge's skill at creating realistic characters and at writing in dialect. Ridge also wrote a series of essays on the American Indian, which have been collected in *A Trumpet of Our Own*.

One of the few novels attributed to an Indian author in the late 19th century is *O-gí-máw-kwe Mit-i-gwá-kí* (*Queen of the Woods*, 1899), which was posthumously published under the name of Simon Pokagon (Potawatomi, 1830–99). The novel, which Pokagon may not have written, combines nostalgic longing for the traditional world of the Potawatomi with fiery attacks on alcohol, which has destroyed many Indian families.

At the end of the century, Emily Pauline Johnson, a Canadian Mohawk (1861–1913), achieved critical acclaim as a poet and performer of her poetry in Canada, the United States, and England. Johnson's father was George Henry Martin, a Mohawk chief, and her mother was Emily Susanna Howells, an English-born cousin of the American writer William Dean Howells. The family's home in Brantford, Ontario, was a gathering spot for Indian and non-Indian visitors.

Johnson's first two volumes of poetry were *White Wampum* (1895) and *Canadian Born* (1903). Her poems from these books and from various periodicals were collected in *Flint and Feather* (1912).

In addition to being a poet, Johnson was one of the first Indian women to publish short fiction. Especially interesting is *The Moccasin Maker* (1913). This book includes a fictional account of the lives of her parents but is primarily a collection of short stories about Indian and non-Indian women in Canada. Many of the stories describe the love of Indian mothers for children and the strength of the pioneer women who established homes for their families despite great hardships. Several focus on the problems of mixed-blood women who are in love with white men. These stories introduce one of the dominant themes of 20th-century American Indian fiction—the mixed blood's search for his or her place in the modern world. Johnson's most popular story with this theme is "A Red Girl's Reasoning," which dramatizes the dilemma of the mixed-blood woman who chooses to remain true to her Indian values even when her decision forces her to leave her white husband, who disparages such ideas.

Another early-20th-century Indian author to gain a large audience was Alexander Posey (Creek, 1873–1907). After graduating from Bacone College in Muskogee, Indian Territory in 1895, Posey held a number of posts as an educator and journalist. Because of his knowledge of both Creek and English, he served as a delegate to many Indian councils. In 1901, Posey began to edit the *Indian Journal*, for which he wrote the "Fus Fixico Letters." Making references to actual Creek elders and writing in Creek-style English, Posey used the words of his character Fus Fixico to satirize the politics of Indian Territory and the United States. The letters were widely reprinted in Indian Territory and in some eastern newspapers as well. In the following excerpt, Fus Fixico dutifully records the wisdom of his friend Hotgun, who neatly summarizes the problems of Indians in dealing with whites:

The missionary he tell the Injin he must lay up treasures in heaven, but he didn't show 'im how to keep body an' soul together on earth an' lay by for the rainy day; an' the school teacher he learn 'im how to read an' shade 'is letters when he write, but didn't teach 'im how to make two blades o' grass grow out o' one; and the philanthropist remind 'him o' the century o' dishonor instead o' the future individual responsibility; an' the government dish out beef an' annuity to 'im instead of a mule an' a plow. Everything like that make the Injin no count, except give jobs to government clerks.

As a youth, Posey wrote poetry, which was collected after his death in *The Poems of Alexander Posey* (1910). Most of the poems are romantic evocations of nature. One exception is "On the Capture and Imprisonment of Crazy Snake." This poem protests the treatment of a Creek leader who was imprisoned because of his opposition to the federal government's policy of allotment. This policy called for the division of tribally owned lands into individually owned tracts and was ultimately responsible for the passing of millions of acres of Indian lands into the hands of whites.

Another Indian author widely read in the early 20th century was Charles Eastman. In addition to writing his autobiographies, Charles and Elaine Eastman, his wife and coauthor, produced both nonfiction and fiction. For the adventure and animal stories in *Red Hunters and the Animal People* (1904), the Eastmans drew on traditional legends and common experiences and observations of Indian hunters. Their *Old Indian Days* (1907) contains stories about warriors and about women. The Eastmans also

reinterpreted traditional stories for children in *Wigwam Evenings: Sioux Folktales Retold* (1909).

Eastman's *Soul of the Indian* (1911) is his most complete statement of his philosophy. Here he describes the Sioux's worship of the "Great Mystery" as "si-

One of the most prolific and widely read Indian authors of the early 20th century, Charles Eastman, in collaboration with his wife, Elaine, wrote several autobiographies and volumes of retellings of traditional stories, a history of American Indians, and a collection of profiles of Indian leaders.

Charles Alexander Eastman
(Ohiyesa)

lent, solitary, free from all self-seeking." He stresses that Indians' faith is not as formulated as that of whites and that, unlike whites, Indians do not force their religion on those unwilling to accept it. Other nonfiction by Eastman includes *The Indian To-day* (1914), a survey of Indian history focusing on Indians' contributions to America and the difficulties of reservation life; and *Indian Heroes and Great Chieftains* (1918), a collection of profiles of Indian leaders that includes anecdotes told to Eastman by the leaders themselves or by their contemporaries.

The best-known Indian author of the 1920s was Will Rogers (Cherokee, 1879–1935). Like Posey, Rogers was a member of a prominent family in Indian Territory. Young Rogers left school in 1898 to became a cowboy and entertainer. By the beginning of World War I, he was a regular on the vaudeville circuit, reaching his greatest success as a performer in the Ziegfeld Follies, a popular stage revue. Roger's famous line "All I know is what I read in the papers" became the preface for his witty commentaries on the national and international scene. These commentaries were collected in his first two books, *Roger-isms: The Cowboy Philosopher on the Peace Conference* and *Roger-isms: The Cowboy Philosopher on Prohibition*, both published in 1919.

Owing to the popularity of Roger's humor, the *New York Times* began syndicating a weekly column written by him in 1922. Four years later, Rogers developed what was to become his

Humorist Will Rogers, who was of Cherokee descent, charmed vaudeville audiences in the 1920s and 1930s with his witty and incisive commentary on national and international affairs.

most influential written medium—a column he called his "daily telegram." It eventually ran in 350 newspapers. During the 1920s, Rogers published a series of books based on these columns and on his observations during his many trips abroad: *Illiterate Digest* (1924); *Letters of a Self-made Diplomat to His President* (1927); *There's not a Bathing Suit in Russia* (1927); and *Ether and Me* (1929). In his writing and in his stage and movie performances, Rogers adopted the role of the wise innocent—a semiliterate cowboy whose bad grammar and exaggerations endeared him to many Americans. Always ready to take on president or prince, big business or government, Rogers was the defender of the underdog. Until he died in a plane crash during a tour of Alaska in 1935, he was the most popular humorist of his age.

The 1920s also saw the publication of the first novel written by an American Indian woman, *Co-ge-we-a, the Half-Blood* (1927). Its author, Mourning Dove (a.k.a. Christine Quintasket, Colville, 1888–1936), spent much of her adult life as a migrant worker in Washington State. Writing in collaboration with Lucullus Virgil McWhorter, founder of *American Anthropologist*, Dove focused her novel on a mixed-blood woman's struggle to find her place and on the need for maintaining tribal culture and oral traditions. Mourning Dove combined these themes with plot elements and characters from popular westerns.

In the novel, the title character initially rejects a mixed-blood cowboy suitor for a "crafty Easterner." But in the end, she recognizes the importance of the values her mixed-blood beau and her Indian grandmother represent. The problems faced by mixed-bloods are especially vivid in the novel's description of one incident that occurs during a Fourth of July celebration: Dressed as a white woman, Cogewea enters and wins a "ladies" horse race, only to be denied the prize by a judge who calls her a squaw. When she then enters a race specifically for Indian women, she is told she has no right to be there because the race is for "Indians and not for breeds!"

The most-published American Indian writer of the 1920s was John Milton Oskison (1874–1947). One-eighth Cherokee, Oskison was raised in Indian Territory, graduated from Stanford, and attended Harvard. He later became an editor and feature writer for *Collier's* magazine and a free-lance writer on finance and Indian affairs. During the 1920s, he published the novels *Wild Harvest* (1925) and *Black Jack Davy* (1926), both of which were "southwesterns" set in Indian Territory just before 1907, when the territory became part of Oklahoma. Oskison's books deal with the surge of white settlers onto Cherokee land near a town called Big Grove.

Oskison's best novel is perhaps *Brothers Three*, a history of the Odell family's efforts to hold on to the farm established by the father, Francis, and his quarter-Cherokee wife, Janet. The novel focuses on the importance of honesty, loyalty, hard work, and thrift and

Mourning Dove's Co-ge-we-a, the Half-Blood *(1927) was the first published novel by an American Indian woman. The book focuses on the struggles of a woman of mixed Indian and white ancestry.*

on the economic and social history of Oklahoma from the turn of the century through the depression. *Brothers Three* demonstrates Oskison's ability to create believable characters and realistic dialogue. Although Indians and issues affecting Indian people are not central to his novels, Oskison did write more explicitly about these subjects in his biography of an early-19th-century Shawnee leader, *Tecumseh and his Times* (1939).

During the 1920s and 1930s, American Indians who attended college increasingly wrote fiction and demonstrated a new sophistication in their works. The most accomplished American Indian novelists to emerge in this decade were John Joseph Mathews (Osage, c. 1894–1979) and D'Arcy McNickle (Cree/Flathead, 1904–77). Unlike most other American writers of the period, their fiction did not focus on economic and social issues. Instead, Mathews and McNickle emphasized the importance of maintaining traditional tribal ways, which had been devastated by U.S. government policies designed to assimilate Indians into mainstream non-Indian society.

Mathews's first book was *Wah' Kon-Tah* (1932). Based on the journal of Major Laban J. Miles, the first government agent, or representative, to live among the Osages, it portrays the Osages' determination to retain their tribal ways despite Laban's attempts to lead them down the white man's road.

Sundown, Mathews's only novel, also examines the impact of non-Indian society on Osage culture. Its protagonist (main character) is Challenge Windzer, a man torn between the beliefs of his full-blood Osage mother, who seeks to maintain tribal traditions, and his mixed-blood father, who advocates assimilation and allotment. Windzer responds by passively rejecting his ancestral past without feeling at home in the white-dominated present. His non-Indian education helps to cut him off from his Indian roots, and this cultural separation is made complete by a brief stint at the University of Oklahoma and in the armed forces during World War I. When he returns home after the war, Windzer inherits enough money from leasing the oil rights to his family's land to destroy his desire either for education or work. Dreaming of glory, Windzer lives in an alcoholic haze, unable to cope with either the Osage or white world. Mathews's next book was a biography entitled *Life and Death of an Oilman: The Career of E. W. Marland* (1952). He also published *The Osages: Children of the Middle Waters* (1961), a lengthy, personalized history of his tribe.

D'Arcy McNickle was a mixed-blood of Cree ancestry on his mother's side and of white ancestry on his father's. When he was a child, however, McNickle, his mother, and his siblings were adopted into the Flathead tribe. McNickle attended the University of Montana, Oxford University in England, and Grenoble University in France. But his experiences in helping to formulate federal Indian policy

Osage historian and novelist John Joseph Mathews in his home in Osage County, Oklahoma. A common theme in all of Mathews's works is his people's determination to resist the influence of white society and maintain their traditions.

proved to be the strongest influence on his writing. From 1936 to 1952, he was an employee of the Bureau of Indian Affairs (BIA), the federal government agency responsible for all matters concerning American Indian tribes. Later, McNickle chaired the Division of Social Sciences at the University of Saskatch-

ewan, cofounded the National Congress of American Indians, and served as the first director of the Center for the History of the American Indian at the Newberry Library in Chicago.

Perhaps the best-written novel by an Indian writer during the 1930s is McNickle's *The Surrounded* (1936). It movingly describes the disintegration of a tribe as a result of the loss of Indian lands to whites and the destruction of tribal religion and values. These themes echoed the concerns of the BIA, which at this time was working to help tribes maintain and recover their traditions through programs outlined in the Indian Reorganization Act of 1934.

Archilde Leon, the protagonist of *The Surrounded*, is the son of a Flathead woman renowned for her Catholic piety and for her refusal to abandon Indian ways. His father is a Spaniard who, even after 40 years of living among Indians, has no insight into their worldviews. Returning to his home after a long absence for a final visit to his parents, Archilde becomes inadvertently involved in two unpremeditated murders that his mother and his girlfriend commit. During the course of these events, his mother and a tribal elder lead him back to the Flathead culture he had rejected. Through this character's return to tribal ways, *The Surrounded* offers more hope for the survival of American Indian culture than does Mathews's *Sundown*.

McNickle's next novel, *The Runner in the Sun* (1954), was written for middle-school readers. Set in the Southwest, the novel describes the culture of the cliff dwellers and the adventures of Salt, a teenage boy who journeys to Mexico in search of a hardy strain of corn that his people can grow in order to save themselves from starvation.

Wind from an Enemy Sky, McNickle's third novel, was published posthu-

mously in 1978. This book examines the effect of the clash of two cultures on groups of people rather than on an individual. The plot contrasts the values of non-Indian culture, symbolized by a dam that cuts off a tribe's water supply and violates a holy place, with those of Indian culture, represented by the medicine bundle of the tribe's most sacred god, Feather Boy. The plot also contrasts the responses by two brothers, one a traditionalist and the other an assimilationist, to the U.S. government's efforts to alter Indian ways of life. As in *The Surrounded*, a murder, in this case of a dam engineer by a young Indian, sets off a chain of events that ends in tragedy.

Although McNickle wrote and published some short stories in his youth, he produced no other novels. Most of his other books are histories: *They Came Here First* (1949); *The Indian Tribes of the United States* (1962); *Indians and Other Americans* (1970), with Harold E. Fey; and *Native American Tribalism* (1973). McNickle also wrote a biography, *Indian Man* (1971), which dealt with the life of Oliver La Farge—the author of fiction and other popular works about Indians and who won the Pulitzer Prize in 1930 for the Navajo love story *Laughing Boy*.

Of the few Indian authors who published poetry during the first half of the 20th century, the most accomplished was Lynn Riggs (Cherokee, 1899–1954). Reared on a farm near what is now Claremore, Oklahoma, Riggs entered the University of Oklahoma in 1920. His only published volume of poetry is *The*

Iron Dish (1930), which includes one poem on a specifically Indian theme, "Santo Domingo Corn Dance." Among the most beautiful of his poems is "Moon," in which Riggs effectively blends imagery of touch, sight, and sound:

What I had waited for in the silken wind
Came over me at last. Radiant I stood
In silver. Silver the pavement's end.
Chaste every poplar, every cottonwood.
A light in the *portales* of the hill
Opened the earth. A cricket shook the air.
On Monte Sol guitars of gold, too still
For music, said a silver prayer.

Riggs is best known as a dramatist. In fact, he was the only Indian author to publish dramas in the early 20th century. His first play produced on Broadway, *Big Lake* (1927), was not a success. Better received were two folk dramas set in Oklahoma that Riggs wrote while living in Paris in 1928. *Borned in Texas*, produced as *Roadside* (1930), portrays a high-spirited cowboy on the run from the law for his brawling and details his attempts to win the love of a sharp-tongued but warmhearted Oklahoma woman. *Green Grow the Lilacs* (1931) was adapted to become the hit musical *Oklahoma!* (1943). Both plays demonstrate Riggs's ability to capture Oklahoma dialect and folk culture. His only drama about Indians is *Cherokee Night* (1936), which deals poignantly with the sense of loss faced by Oklahoma mixed-bloods living near Claremore in the early 20th century as they grow away from their Cherokee heritage.

Although he continued to write plays, Riggs did not equal the success of his early work. He did, however, serve as a free-lance screenwriter on such films as *The Garden of Allah* and *The Plainsman*. Riggs also served as guest author and director of drama at Northwestern University and the University of Iowa.

During the 1940s, few books by Indian authors were published. This was due in part to the paper shortage caused by World War II, which severely curtailed all publishing. Involvement in the war effort or service in the army also interrupted the literary careers of many Indian authors. Most of the books by Indians that were published during this period were cultural histories or autobiographies.

Among these authors was Ella C. Deloria (1888–1971). A Sioux and the daughter of an Episcopalian deacon, Deloria was raised on the Standing Rock Indian Reservation in North and South Dakota. After graduating from Teachers College in New York City in 1915, she served as a YWCA health education secretary and physical education teacher. From 1927 to 1942, Deloria assisted Franz Boas, a well-known anthropologist, as a research specialist. At his urging, she translated and edited Sioux written texts. Deloria is best known for her *Dakota Texts* (1932) and *Dakota Grammar* (1941). Another of her books, *Speaking of Indians* (1944), is a detailed account of how the Sioux retained traditional values after their settlement on reservations.

Dramatist Lynn Riggs, 1922. Riggs is best known for writing Green Grow the Lilacs *(1931), on which the book for the hit musical* Oklahoma! *was based.*

Deloria also wrote a novel, *Waterlily*. Although it was completed in draft form by 1944, it was not published until 1988. Told from a woman's perspective, the work is an affecting portrayal of 19th-century Sioux life. The story traces the life of the title character from birth through childhood, marriage, widowhood, childbirth, and remarriage. In the course of the novel, Deloria introduces the reader to Dakota camp life, rituals, kinship systems, and customs. The author also describes in detail the ceremonies that the nine-year-old Waterlily's family holds for her when they designate her a "beloved child," a special status for those who, as adults, must make hospitality their first concern. Deloria gives a touching portrait of the education and rearing of Sioux children. The contrast between how children are raised among the Sioux and among whites is made clear in the following passage, in which a Sioux character expresses horror at whites' treatment of their children:

Listen! those people actually detest their children! You should see them—slapping their little ones' faces and lashing their poor little buttocks to make them cry! Why, almost any time of day if you walk near the stockade you can hear the soldiers' wives screaming at their children. Yes, they thoroughly scold them. I have never seen children treated so. . . . Only if a woman is crazy might she turn on her own child, not knowing what she did.

During the 1950s, many American Indians devoted their energies to combating new threats to the tribes rather than to writing creative works. Under pressure to end the "Indian problem," politicians abandoned their support of the federal programs of the 1930s that supported tribalism. Particularly significant was the passage in 1953 of House Concurrent Resolution 108, which began the campaign to terminate the federal government's role in Indian affairs and to integrate American Indians into mainstream American society. To achieve this, the United States tried to end its financial responsibilities to tribes; convert tribally owned reservations, such as those of the Klamath and Menominee, into private property; and relocate reservation Indians to cities. American Indians strongly resisted this new onslaught on their traditional cultures and societies. Their resistance is exemplified in the long legal battle waged by the Menominee. Not until 1973 did they regain reservation status by becoming wards of the government again. The renewed sense of tribalism and pride in Indian culture that emerged among American Indians during their struggles with the government would stimulate numbers to become writers in the coming decades. ▲

N. Scott Momaday, author of the 1969 Pulitzer Prize–winning novel
House Made of Dawn.

A LITERARY RENAISSANCE:
1968–THE PRESENT

The revitalization of Indian pride in the 1960s ushered in an era of literary creativity unequaled in the history of Indian literature written in English. The quality and quantity of fiction and poetry produced by Indians became greater than ever before. The writer whose work began this renaissance was N. Scott Momaday. After the publication of his highly praised novel *House Made of Dawn* (1968) and autobiography *The Way to Rainy Mountain* (1969) [see page 70], Momaday became the most influential American Indian writer of the late 1960s and early 1970s.

House Made of Dawn won the Pulitzer Prize and received more critical acclaim than any previous Indian novel. Momaday's book emphasized the problems of Indians in contemporary society and the importance of oral tradition and ritual and used memory to structure its plot. The novel focuses on Abel, who becomes alienated from his Jemez Pueblo and its traditions. During an od-

yssey that takes him to Europe as a soldier during World War II and later to Los Angeles, Abel conquers a variety of enemies in his quest to achieve a sense of place, tribe, and self. Momaday's *Ancient Child* (1989) also focuses on its hero's ritual journey toward reunification with his tribal heritage. Here, the quest by Lock Setman, a middle-aged, mixed-blood artist, culminates in his transformation into a bear, a theme common in ancient Indian myths. Momaday is also a poet whose collections include *The Gourd Dancer* (1976).

Leslie Marmon Silko (Laguna, b. 1948) is another widely read contemporary Indian storyteller. Silko, who is of mixed Laguna-Mexican-white ancestry, was raised in Laguna Pueblo, New Mexico, and graduated from the University of New Mexico. Her novel *Ceremony* (1977) was written in response to Momaday's *House Made of Dawn*. Like Momaday, she examines the life of a Pueblo World War II veteran and uses his quest for meaning as her central theme. Tayo, an illegitimate mixed-blood, cherishes the Laguna culture rejected by his progressive cousin, Rocky. But the death of Rocky and his own experiences in the Philippine jungle during the war cause Tayo to suffer a psychological breakdown. His memory of Laguna stories and his participation in a variety of rituals heal him. At the end of the novel, he is reunited with his people.

Silko also focuses on Indian themes in her short stories, collected with her poetry and autobiographical commentary in *Storyteller* (1981). One story, "Yellow Woman," is a modern version of a type of Pueblo myth that tells of a woman who goes to a river to fill her water jars and there meets a handsome stranger. Another, entitled "Lullaby," describes the heartbreak a Navajo woman suffers as a result of her children being sent away to school. Silko's keen sense of humor is expressed in two stories: "The Man to Send Rainclouds," in which traditional Pueblo Indians hoodwink a naive local priest into sprinkling holy water on the body of a dead relative, a tribal ritual performed to ensure rain; and "Coyote Holds a Full House in His Hand," in which a lusty Laguna trickster convinces some trusting Hopi women that he is a medicine man.

A second Indian writer to gain national recognition in the 1970s was James Welch (Blackfeet/Gros Ventre, b. 1940). In his first novel, *Winter in the Blood* (1975), Welch traces the efforts of a nameless hero to learn or remember the truth about his fierce Blackfeet grandmother's early life, the identity of his grandfather, his parents' relationship, and the deaths of his brother and father. Using a spare style that combines tragedy with humor, Welch creates powerful depictions of reservation life and characterizations of women.

Some aspects of the plot of Welch's second novel, *The Death of Jim Loney* (1979), parallel those of *Winter in the Blood*: A protagonist in his thirties cannot integrate the different parts of his

The book jacket of Tracks, *which was a best-seller in 1988.*

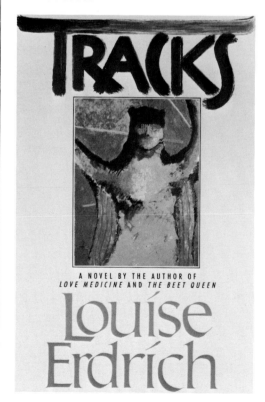

life or the people who enter and leave it. In *The Death of Jim Loney*, the hero tries to find out about his Indian mother and white father, who abandoned their children. Because he cannot forget the past, he grows unable to organize his life. By the novel's end, the protagonist finds release from his psychological dilemma in an act that brings about his own death.

Far different from Welch's early novels is *Fools Crow* (1986). Here the author vividly describes the impact of white settlement on a Montana band of Blackfeet in the 1870s and gives a colorful and moving account of tribal life during that period. The central character is Fools Crow, a young man who is a traditionalist and avoids whites as much as possible. In the course of describing the maturation of Fools Crow, Welch recounts the character's experiences as a warrior and later as a shaman. Welch weaves oral narratives and literature from ceremonies into his detailed account of traditional Blackfeet life.

Among the most prolific American Indian authors is Gerald Vizenor (Ojibwa, b. 1934). Several of his works combine fiction and nonfiction: *Wordarrows* (1978), *Earthdivers* (1981), and *The People Named the Chippewa* (1984). In all of these books, Vizenor incisively describes the wounds suffered by Indians as a result of the cultural conflicts between the white and tribal worlds. Particularly powerful are his portraits of real Indian people who have been overcome by the pressure of adapting to non-Indian society. One example from *Earthdivers* is the story of Dane Michael White, a 13-year-old Sioux runaway who hanged himself in a Minnesota jail while the courts tried to decide whether to place him in a foster home or allow him to live with his grandmother.

Vizenor has also written three novels—*Darkness in Saint Louis Bearheart* (1978), which was retitled *Bearheart* in the 1990 edition; *Griever: An American Money King in China* (1987); and *The Trickster of Liberty: Tribal Heirs to a Wild Baronage at Petronia* (1988). All satirize Indian and non-Indian societies and incorporate versions of trickster myths. Vizenor's unpublished screenplay of the film *Harold of Orange* also focuses on a trickster character.

Another prolific Ojibwa novelist is Louise Erdrich (b. 1954). Born in North Dakota, Erdrich received her B.A. from Dartmouth College and her M.A. from Johns Hopkins. Her three novels—*Love Medicine* (1984), *The Beet Queen* (1986), and *Tracks* (1988)—were written in collaboration with her husband, Michael Dorris. Each book weaves an intricate web of relationships among members of individual families and family groups of Indians, mixed-bloods, and whites. Each novel also incorporates an image: water—*Love Medicine*, air—*The Beet Queen*, and earth—*Tracks*. All of Erdrich's novels use multiple narrators, each of whom tells a part of the story.

Tracks deals with the years between 1912 and 1919. The central character is Fleur Pillager, who survives the death of her family in an epidemic, near

Wife and husband Louise Erdrich and Michael Dorris collaborated on the novel trilogy that includes Love Medicine, The Beet Queen, *and* Tracks.

drownings, and rape to become a figure of mythic power. She is reared by Nanapush, a witty storyteller and keen observer who is named after the Ojibwa culture hero.

The Beet Queen, set in the off-reservation town of Argus, covers the years from 1932 to 1972, during which time the farmers living near the town switched from growing wheat to raising sugar beets. Exploring the themes of abandonment and obsessive love, this novel focuses on the relationships among three women, one Indian and two white.

Love Medicine is a collection of interconnected stories that take place between 1934 and 1983. They powerfully and humorously portray through several generations the families of Nector Kashpaw, a mixed-blood man, and the two women he loves: his wife, Marie Lazarre Kashpaw, and his mistress, Lulu Nanapush Lamartine.

In addition to working with Louise Erdrich, Michael Dorris (Modoc, b. 1945) is an author in his own right. Reared in Kentucky, Washington, Idaho, and Montana, Dorris received his B.A. from Georgetown University and his M.Phil. from Yale University. Formerly a professor of Native American studies and anthropology at Dartmouth College, he is now a full-time writer. His first novel, *A Yellow Raft on Blue Water* (1989), is set on a Montana reservation and tells the story of three generations of women torn apart by secrets but bound by kinship. One of these narrators is 15-year-old Rayona, whose mother is Indian and whose absent father is African American. The novel is the first by an Indian author to deal with a mixed-blood character of this heritage. The book combines strong characterization with scenes that are both poignant and farcical. With Louise Erdrich, Dorris has completed a second novel, *The Crown of Columbus* (1991). He has also written *The Broken Cord: A Family's On-Going Struggle with Fetal Alcohol Syndrome* (1989), which discusses an illness that sometimes affects children whose mothers drink alcohol during pregnancy. This work of nonfiction describes the effects of the syndrome on his and Erdrich's adopted son, Abel.

Martin Cruz Smith (Senecu del Sur/ Yaqui, b. 1942) is an Indian author who has written exclusively in the mystery genre. Born in Reading, Pennsylvania, Smith received his B.A. from the University of Pennsylvania. He subsequently worked for the *Philadelphia Daily News* and *Magazine Management* before becoming a full-time writer. Both his commercially successful *Nightwing* (1977) and his highly praised *Stallion Gate* (1986) tell of Indian protagonists who serve in overseas wars and, upon returning to their homelands, find that they feel separated from their people and their traditions. Both of these novels' heroes also confront forces capable of destroying humankind: an invasion of Mexican bats in *Nightwing* and the atomic bomb in *Stallion Gate*. With his 1981 thriller *Gorky Park*, Smith departs from Indian themes. Set in Moscow, this taut novel, which was made into a

Martin Cruz Smith's popular thrillers include Gorky Park *(1981) and its sequel,* Polar Star *(1989).*

movie, chronicles the efforts of detective Arkady Renko to solve a bizarre murder and an American businessman's plot to undercut a monopoly on the sale of Russian minks. The sequel, *Polar Star*, is an equally absorbing novel that recounts the adventures of the now banished Renko, who works aboard a fish factory ship named the *Polar Star*. In this exciting book, Renko must not only solve the murder of a female Russian shipworker but also outwit the attempts on his own life made by another worker whom the detective had previously sent to prison.

Combining mystery and Oklahoma Indian history is *Mean Spirit* (1990) by Linda Hogan (Chickasaw, b. 1947). The author earned her B.A. and M.A. from the University of Colorado. Formerly associate professor of Native American and American studies at the University of Minnesota, Hogan now writes full-time. Her powerful novel describes an Osage Indian community during the oil boom of the 1920s. It is a fictionalized account of historical events surrounding the murders of Native Americans, especially women, in Osage country and includes both real and fictional characters. The protagonist is Nola Blanket, a teenager whose mother is murdered because of her oil wealth, whose father-in-law steals her money, and whose fear leads her to the false conclusion that her husband plans to kill her. The murders are solved by Stacey Red Hawk, a Sioux FBI agent and medicine man. Throughout, Hogan interweaves Osage religious beliefs, stories, and customs.

Another Indian author of a mystery is Anna Walters (Otoe/Pawnee, b. 1946). Born in Oklahoma and educated at the Institute of American Indian Arts in Santa Fe, New Mexico, Walters now works for the Navajo Community College Press in Tsaile, Arizona. Her first novel, *Ghost Singer* (1988), is an intriguing blend of mystery and history that describes the long-term impact of the enslavement of the members of a Navajo family by Mexicans.

Another contemporary American Indian novelist is Thomas King (Cherokee, b. 1943). King received degrees from California State University and a Ph.D. from the University of Utah. He is now on the faculty of the Department of American Studies at the University of Minnesota. His *Medicine River* (1990) is set in a fictional town located near the Blood Reserve in Alberta, Canada. The novel traces the efforts of the mixed-blood protagonist, Will, to learn more about himself and his family. A humorous catalyst for much of the action is Will's friend Harlen Bigbear, who is full of misguided ideas and rambling stories.

Two authors have written novels from a feminist perspective. Paula Gunn Allen (Laguna/Sioux, b. 1939) uses the ritual quest as the motif for her book *The Woman Who Owned the Shadows* (1983). Raised in Cubero, New Mexico, Allen is Laguna/Sioux on her mother's side and Lebanese on her father's. She received her B.A. and M.F.A. from the

In addition to being a novelist and poet, Paula Gunn Allen is the author of The Sacred Hoop, *a feminist study of American Indian literature and culture.*

University of Oregon and her Ph.D. in American Studies from the University of New Mexico. She is now professor of English at the University of California, Los Angeles. *The Woman Who Owned the Shadows* focuses on the journey toward spiritual rebirth of Epiphanie Atencio, a half blood who feels at home neither in the Southwest nor in San Francisco.

Janet Campbell Hale (Coeur d'Alene/Kootenai; b. 1947) was raised on the Coeur-d'Alene reservation in northern Idaho; she received her B.A. from the University of California,

Many of the works of Choctaw poet Jim Barnes exhibit the strong sense of place traditionally found in American Indian oral literatures.

Berkeley, and her M.A. in English from the University of California, Davis. Her novel *The Jailing of Cecelia Capture* (1985) portrays an alcoholic urban Indian woman who is separated from her husband and children and is trying to rebuild her life. Hale's first novel, *Owl's Song* (1974), focuses on the experiences of Billy, an adolescent who copes with reservation alcoholism, teenage suicide, and urban schools that are unprepared to deal with Indian students. It is one of the few works about an adolescent urban Indian.

Forrest Carter's (a.k.a. Asa, Cherokee, 1925–79) *The Education of Little Tree* (1976) is a fictionalized autobiography written for young people. It tells of an orphaned Cherokee boy raised in the Tennessee mountains by his traditional grandparents and temporarily separated from them by state authorities. Carter also wrote several westerns: *The Rebel Outlaw, Josey Wales* (1973); *The Vengeance Trail of Josey Wales* (1976); and *Watch for Me on the Mountain* (1978).

Another author who has written fiction with a teenage hero is Markoosie (b. 1942), a Canadian Inuit who has worked as a pilot. His short novel *Harpoon of the Hunter* (1970) is one of the few works of fiction by an Inuit. In vivid detail Markoosie traces the harrowing adventures of 16-year-old Kamik as the member of a party trying to kill a wounded, rabid bear. After his father and the other members of the hunting party are killed by another bear, Kamik undergoes great hardships as he tries to make his way back to his people.

Although Indian authors have increasingly turned to writing fiction, poetry is their favored medium. Since the late 1960s, the number of Indian poets has grown steadily. The works of these many artists vary considerably in both form and content.

Contemporary Indian poets sometimes use traditional chants and songs to create highly individualistic verse. In some of his poems, Simon Ortiz (Acoma, b. 1941) combines traditional song techniques of repetition and incremental development with political protest, exemplified in the following excerpt from "It Will Come" in *Fight Back*:

Where from is it thundering.
Thundering, the People working.
Thundering, the People's voices.
Thundering, the movement of the
    struggle.
Thundering, the power of the Land.
Thundering, the coming Rain.
It will come, it will come.

Many Indian writers incorporate tribal myths into their poems. For instance, Ortiz and another well-known Indian poet, Paula Gunn Allen, have included versions of emergence origin stories in their work. Allen gives the Laguna myth in "Creation Story" and Simon Ortiz tells the Acoma story in "Creation, According to Coyote." Ortiz also includes the trickster Coyote in his version.

In "The Significance of a Water Animal," Ray Young Bear (Mesquakie, b. 1950) describes the Mesquakie origin myth of an earth-diver who dives beneath floodwaters to bring up the bit of dirt that becomes the earth. (The Mesquakie of Tama, Iowa, are known as the Red Earth People).

A certain voice of *Reassurance*
tells me a story of a water animal
diving to make land available.
Next, from the Creator's
own heart and flesh
O ki ma was made:
The progeny of divine
leaders. And then
from the Red Earth
came the rest of us.

Leslie Silko retells numerous myths in the poems that are interspersed in her novel *Ceremony*, several of which are reprinted in her book *Storyteller*. Among these is a series of poems—including "Cottonwood," "Yellow Woman," "What Whirlwind Man Told Kochininako," and "Storytelling"—that retell ancient and modern stories about a woman's meeting with a good-looking stranger.

The most popular myths retold by contemporary authors are modern versions of the activities of a trickster, usually called Coyote. In *Storyteller* Silko includes two poems, "Coyotes and the Stro'ro'ka Dancers" and "Toe'Osh," that are modern versions of trickster myths. In "Telling about Coyote," Ortiz describes how the trickster lost his beautiful fur coat in a poker game. Louise Erdrich recounts stories about the Ojibwa culture hero and trickster in her "Old Man Potchikoo" poems in her collection *Jacklight* (1984). Peter Blue Cloud (Mohawk, b. 1935) devotes *Elderberry Flute Song* to contemporary Coyote poems and tales.

Another common theme in contemporary Indian poetry is a sense of loss of tribal roots. This feeling is often associated with a specific place that is part of the history of the poet's tribe. Duane Niatum (Klallam, b. 1938) expresses this theme in the following lines from the title poem of *Digging Out the Roots*:

Today I follow my spirit into the ruins
of my Klallam ancestors, N'huia'wulsh,
their white fir village, count the rainy
    seasons
Since grandfather fell in the brush like
    first cedar,
Regions of fern and snail. I return
To carve red moon out of my native sky.

Closeness to nature and animals is another common subject of Indian poems. In her poem "I Was Sleeping Where the Black Oaks Move," Erdrich combines a sense of the mythic past, identification with place, and sensitive description of nature. The poem describes the impact of a flood on a nest of herons and on trees near the river on the Turtle Mountain Indian Reservation in North Dakota:

When at last it was over, the long
    removal,
they had all become the same dry wood.
We walked among them, the branches
whitening in the raw sun.
Above us drifted herons,
alone, hoarse-voiced, broken
settling their beaks among the hollows.

Grandpa said, There are the ghosts of the
    tree people,
moving above us, unable to take their
    rest.

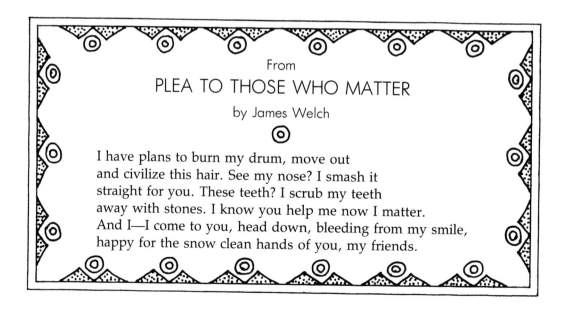

From

PLEA TO THOSE WHO MATTER

by James Welch

I have plans to burn my drum, move out
and civilize this hair. See my nose? I smash it
straight for you. These teeth? I scrub my teeth
away with stones. I know you help me now I matter.
And I—I come to you, head down, bleeding from my smile,
happy for the snow clean hands of you, my friends.

Sometimes now, we dream our way back
   to the heron dance.
Their long wings are bending the air
into circles through which they fall.
They rise again in shifting wheels.
How long must we live in the broken
   figures
their necks make, narrowing the sky.

Like Indian novelists, many Indian poets use their art to explore the problems of identity that mixed-bloods face and the sense of displacement that Indians living in urban areas encounter. Linda Hogan (Chickasaw, b. 1947) focuses on the differences between the Indian and white sides of her heritage in "The Truth Is." She dramatizes the issue by explaining that she puts her Chickasaw hand in her left pants pocket and her white hand in the right. In several of his poems, Barney Bush (Shawnee/Cayuga, b. 1937) depicts the self-destruction that Indians often suffer in the city. In "I think of the lights," he describes how some urban Indians destroy their lives with alcohol and pills and concludes:

Explain this to your ancestors
when you finally have
to face them
and take your first
true walk
and last vision of what
your lives could have
been
in the tall pines
along the clear and
cooling streams
in the aspen scented
air of the mountains

Another frequent theme is the pain Indians feel when forced to assimilate into mainstream non-Indian society. Diane Glancy's (Cherokee, b. 1941) "Female Seminary, Tahlequah, Indian Territory, 1850–1905" and Erdrich's "Indian Boarding School: The Runaways" describe the experiences of Indian children taken from their parents and sent far away to Indian boarding schools, where they were taught the ways of whites. Indians' sense of anger at the changes they and their culture have endured is expressed by James Welch in the lines on the facing page from his "Plea to Those Who Matter."

The family has long been a source of strength that Indians have drawn on in order to withstand others' attempts to alter their culture. The importance placed on family is reflected in many poems. For instance, Simon Ortiz includes numerous poems about children and parents in *Going for the Rain* and *The Good Journey*. In "Father's Song," Ortiz describes a childhood memory of how his father stopped plowing one day to show his son a family of mice.

Very gently, he scooped tiny pink animals
into the palm of his hand
and told me to touch them.
We took them to the edge
of the field and put them in the shade
of a sand moist clod.

I remember the very softness
of cool and warm sand and tiny alive
   mice
and my father saying things.

Joy Harjo, whose books include What Moon Drove Me to This *and* In Mad Love and War, *is one of the many talented female Indian poets to emerge in recent years.*

In their works, Indian women writers frequently focus on the roles of women, especially of those in their own family. Often they write about their grandmothers, the relatives who in many Indian societies traditionally helped raise children and educate them in tribal traditions. Especially moving is Allen's "Grandma's Dying Poem," in which she reflects on her relationship with her dead grandmother:

She's somehow what your life has been
all along,
you realize—your life has been
a mirror of her ways, the reflection
slightly different by small changes
time and fashion make

Although many American Indian authors have written fiction and poetry, few have written drama. Among them are Gerald Vizenor and Linda Hogan, both of whom are better known for their work in other genres. One contemporary Indian author who writes plays exclusively is Hanay Geiogamah (Kiowa, b.1945). His *New Native American Drama: Three Plays* includes the satiric dramas *Foghorn*, *49*, and *Body Indian*.

The most prolific Indian writer of nonfiction prose is Vine Deloria, Jr. (Sioux, b. 1933). Born in South Dakota, Deloria received his B.S. from Iowa State University, his M.Th. from the Lutheran School of Theology, and his J.D. from the University of Colorado. Formerly executive director of the National Congress of American Indians and chairman of the Institute for Development of Indian Law, Deloria has also been vice-chairman of the American Indian Resource Association and worked with the United Scholarship Service. He is currently professor of Native American studies and political science at the University of Arizona.

Deloria's keen wit and sharp satire are exemplified by *Custer Died for Your Sins* (1969) and *We Talk, You Listen* (1970). Both volumes demonstrate political insight into the problems of contemporary Indian life. Deloria has also written numerous books on Indian-white relations and Indian religion.

For contemporary Indian authors, the written word is a tool that allows them to work in new genres unknown to their ancestors and to preserve their literary heritage and share it with others. American Indian literatures have therefore become one of the most effective means Indian people have of maintaining the continuity of their culture despite centuries of rapid change. In "It Doesn't End, Of Course," Simon Ortiz beautifully summarizes the inspiration Indian culture has given tribal people to live and to create since time immemorial:

It doesn't end.
In all growing
from all earths
to all skies,
in all touching
all things,
in all soothing
the aches of all years,
it doesn't end. ▲

WORKS CITED

p. 13, N. Scott Momaday, "The Native Voice," in *The Columbia Literary History of the United States,* ed. Emory Elliott (New York: Columbia University Press, 1988), 5–15.

p. 14, Laura Coltelli, ed., *Winged Words: Native American Writers Speak* (Lincoln: University of Nebraska Press, 1990).

p. 16, Charles A. Eastman, *Indian Boyhood* (1902; reprint, Greenwich, CT: Fawcett Books, 1972).

p. 17, Larry Evers and Felipe M. Molina, *Yaqui Deer Songs,* Sun Tracks Series, no. 14 (Tucson: University of Arizona Press, 1986).

p. 18, Leslie Marmon Silko, *Ceremony* (1977; reprint, New York: Penguin Books, 1986).

p. 20, N. Scott Momaday, *The Way to Rainy Mountain* (Albuquerque: University of New Mexico Press, 1969).

p. 20, Black Elk and John G. Neihardt. *Black Elk Speaks* (1932; reprint, Lincoln: University of Nebraska Press, 1972).

p. 21, Paula Gunn Allen, *The Sacred Hoop: Recovering the Feminine in American Indian Traditions* (Boston: Beacon Press, 1975).

p. 27, Washington Mathews, "The Night Chant," in *Memoirs of the American Museum of Natural History* (1902; reprint, New York: AMS, 1974).

p. 28, John Bierhorst, ed., *Four Masterworks of American Indian Literature* (1974; reprint, Tucson: University of Arizona Press, 1984).

p. 30, Marcia Herndon, *Native American Music* (Norwood, PA: Norwood, 1980).

p. 31, Frances Densmore, ed., *Chippewa Music* (1910; reprint as *Chippewa Music* 1, Music Reprint Series, New York: Da Capo Press, 1972).

p. 32, Evers and Molina. *Yaqui Deer Songs.*

p. 33, Herbert Joseph Spinden, ed. and trans., *Songs of the Tewa* (1933; reprint, Santa Fe: Sun Stone, 1976).

p. 34, Ruth M. Underhill, *Singing for Power* (1938; reprint, Berkeley: University of California Press, 1976).

p. 34, James Mooney, "Ghost Dance Religion and the Sioux Outbreak of 1980," in *Annual Report of the Bureau of American Ethnology* 14, no. 2 (1892–93), Classics in Anthropology Series (1896; reprint, New York: Dover, 1976).

p. 35–36, E. Adamson Hoebel, "Song Duels Among the Eskimo," in *Law and Warfare: Studies in the Anthropology of Conflict,* ed. Paul Bohannan (Garden City, NY: Natural History, 1967), 255–62.

p. 36, George Copway, *Life, Letters and Speeches,* 2nd ed. (New York: Benedict, 1850).

p. 36, Densmore, *Chippewa Music.*

p. 36, Frances Densmore, *Teton Sioux Music* (1918; reprint, New York: Da Capo Press, 1972).

p. 36, Maurice Boyd, *Kiowa Voices, Vol. I: Ceremonial Dance, Ritual and Song* (Fort Worth: Texas Christian University Press, 1981).

p. 37, Richard Lewis, *I Breathe a New Song: Poems of the Eskimo* (New York: Simon & Schuster, 1971).

p. 37, Ruth Bunzel, ed., "Zuni Ritual Poetry," in *Annual Report of the Bureau of American Ethnology* 47 (1929–30), 611–835.

p. 39, George Copway, *Traditional History and Characteristic Sketches of the Ojibway Nation* (1851; reprint, New York: AMS, 1977).

p. 40, Virginia Beavert, *The Way It Was: Anaku Iwacha: Yakima Legends* (Yakima, WA: Franklin Press, 1974).

p. 42, John Stands in Timber, *Cheyenne Memoirs* (New Haven: Yale University Press, 1967).

p. 44, Dean Saxton and Lucille Saxton, eds., *O'othom Hoho'ok A'agitha: Legends and Lore of the Papago and Pima Indians* (Tucson: University of Arizona Press, 1973).

p. 60, Michael K. Foster, *From the Earth to Beyond the Sky: An Ethnographical Approach to Four Iroquois Speech Events,* National Museum of Man, Mercury Series, Canadian Ethnology Service Paper no. 20 (Ottawa: National Museums of Canada, 1974).

p. 61, Theodore J. Balgooyen, "The Plains Indian as Public Speaker," in *Landmarks in Western Oratory*, ed. David H. Grover (Laramie, WY: Graduate School and Western Speech Association, 1968).

p. 62, Peter Nabokov, ed., *Native American Testimony: An Anthology of Indian and White Relations. First Encounter to Dispossession* (New York: Harper & Row, 1979).

p. 62, Virginia Armstrong, ed., *I Have Spoken: American History Through the Voices of the Indians* (Athens: Swallow-Ohio University Press, 1971).

p. 63, Jarold W. Ramsey, *Coyote Was Going There: Indian Literature of Oregon County* (Seattle: University of Washington Press, 1977).

p. 64, William Apes, *A Son of the Forest: The Experience of William Apes, a Native of the Forest.,* 2nd ed. (New York: G. E. Bunce, 1831).

p. 66, Sarah Winnemuca [Hopkins], *Life Among the Piutes: Their Wrongs and Claims,* ed. Mrs. Horace Mann (1833; reprint, Bishop, CA: Chalfant, 1969).

p. 76, John Rollin Ridge, *The Life and Adventures of Joaquin Murieta* (1854; reprint, Norman: University of Oklahoma Press, 1977).

pp. 77–78, Alexander Posey, column in *Holderville Times,* 19 June 1906.

p. 85, Lynn Riggs [Rolla], *The Iron Dish* (1932; reprint in *This Book, This Hill, These People: Poems by Lynn Riggs,* Tulsa, OK: Lynn Chase, 1982).

p. 87, Ella C. Deloria, *Waterlily* (Lincoln: University of Nebraska Press, 1988).

p. 97, Simon Ortiz, "Fight Back: For the Sake of the People, for the Sake of the Land," *INAD Literary Journal* 1, no. 1 (1980).

p. 97, Ray Young Bear, *Invisible Musician* (Duluth, MN: Holy Cow! Press, 1990).

p. 98, Duane Niatum, *Digging Out the Roots* (New York: Harper & Row, 1977).

pp. 98–99, Louise Erdrich, *Jacklight: Poems* (New York: Henry Holt, 1984).

p. 98, James Welch, *Riding the Earthboy 40* (1971; rev. ed. New York: Harper & Row, 1975).

p. 99, Barney Bush, *My Horse and a Jukebox.* Native American Series, no. 4. (Los Angeles: University of California, American Indian Studies Center, 1979).

p. 99, Simon Ortiz, *Going for the Rain* (New York: Harper & Row, 1976).

p. 101, Paula Gunn Allen, *Skins and Bones: Poems 1979–81.* (New Mexico: West End Press, 1988).

p. 101, Ortiz, *Going for the Rain.*

BIBLIOGRAPHY

Bibliographies and Guides to Research

Brumble, H. David III, comp. *An Annotated Bibliography of American Indian and Eskimo Autobiographies*. Lincoln: University of Nebraska Press, 1981.

Clements, William M., and Frances M. Malpezzi, comps. *Native American Folklore, 1879–1979: An Annotated Bibliography*. Athens: Swallow–Ohio University Press, 1984.

Colonnese, Tom, and Louis Owens, comps. *American Indian Novelists: An Annotated Critical Bibliography*. New York: Garland, 1985.

Littlefield, Daniel L., Jr. (Cherokee), and James M. Parins, comps. *American Indian and Alaska Native Newspapers and Periodicals, 1826–1924*. Westport, CT: Greenwood Press, 1984.

————. *A Bibliography of Native American Writers, 1771–1924*. Metuchen, NJ: Scarecrow Press, 1985.

Marken, Jack, comp. *The American Indian: Language and Literature*. Arlington Heights, IL: AHM, 1978.

Ruoff, A. LaVonne Brown. *American Indian Literatures: An Introduction, Bibliographic Review, and Selected Bibliography*. New York: Modern Language Association, 1990.

Stensland, Anna, comp. *Literature by and About the American Indian: An Annotated Bibliography for Junior and Senior High School Students*. Urbana, IL: National Council of Teachers of English, 1973.

————. *Literature by and About the American Indian: An Annotated Bibliography*, 2nd ed. Urbana, IL: National Council of Teachers of English, 1979.

Anthologies

Allen, Paula Gunn (Laguna/Sioux), ed. *Spider Woman's Granddaughters: Traditional Tales and Contemporary Writing by Native American Women*. Boston: Beacon Press, 1989.

Armstrong, Virginia, ed. *I Have Spoken: American History Through the Voices of the Indians*. Athens: Swallow–Ohio University Press, 1971.

Bruchac, Joseph, III (Abenaki), ed. *Songs from This Earth on Turtle's Back: Contemporary American Indian Poetry*. Greenfield Center, NY: Greenfield Review Literary Center, 1983.

Evers, Larry, ed. *The South Corner of Time: Hopi, Navajo, Papago, Yaqui Tribal Literature*. Tucson: University of Arizona Press, 1980.

Gedalof, Robin, ed. *Paper Stays Put: A Collection of Inuit Writing.* Edmonton, Alberta, Canada: Hurtig Publications, 1980.

Green, Rayna (Cherokee), ed. *That's What She Said: Contemporary Poetry and Fiction by Native American Women.* Bloomington: University of Indiana Press, 1984.

Hobson, Geary (Cherokee), ed. *The Remembered Earth: An Anthology of Contemporary Native American Literature.* Albuquerque: University of New Mexico Press, 1980.

Nabokov, Peter, ed. *Native American Testimony: An Anthology of Indian and White Relations: First Encounter to Dispossession.* New York: Harper & Row, 1979.

Niatum, Duane (Klallam), ed. *Carriers of the Dream Wheel: Contemporary Native American Poetry.* San Francisco: Harper & Row, 1975.

———. *Harper's Anthology of 20th Century Native American Poetry.* New York: Harper & Row, 1988.

Ortiz, Simon J. (Acoma), ed. *Earth Power Coming: Short Fiction in Native American Literature.* Tsaile, AZ: Navajo Community College Press, 1983.

Peyer, Bernd, ed. *The Singing Spirit: Early Short Stories by North American Indians.* Tucson: University of Arizona Press, 1989.

Rosen, Kenneth, ed. *The Man to Send Rain Clouds: Contemporary Stories by American Indians.* New York: Viking, 1974.

———. *Voices of the Rainbow: Contemporary Poetry by American Indians.* New York: Viking Penguin, 1975.

Swann, Brian, and Arnold Krupat, eds. *I Tell You Now: Autobiographical Essays by Native American Writers.* Lincoln: University of Nebraska Press, 1987.

Velie, Alan R., ed. *American Indian Literature: An Anthology.* Norman: University of Oklahoma Press, 1979.

Criticism

Allen, Paula Gunn (Laguna/Sioux). *The Sacred Hoop: Recovering the Feminine in American Indian Traditions.* Boston: Beacon Press, 1986.

Bataille, Gretchen M., and Kathleen Mullen Sands. *American Indian Women: Telling Their Lives.* Lincoln: University of Nebraska Press, 1984.

Bruchac, Joseph, III, (Abenaki) ed. *Survival This Way: Interviews with American Indian Poets.* Tucson: University of Arizona Press, 1987.

Brumble, H. David, III. *American Indian Autobiography.* Berkeley: University of California Press, 1988.

Coltelli, Laura, ed. *Winged Words: Native American Writers Speak.* Lincoln: University of Nebraska, 1990.

Krupat, Arnold. *For Those Who Come After: A Study of Native American Autobiography.* Berkeley: University of California Press, 1985.

————. *The Voice in the Margin: Native American Literature and the Canon.* Berkeley: University of California Press, 1989.

Larson, Charles R. *American Indian Fiction.* Albuquerque: University of New Mexico Press, 1978.

Lincoln, Kenneth. *Native American Renaissance.* 2nd ed, rev. Los Angeles: University of California Press, 1985.

Swann, Brian, ed. *Smoothing the Ground: Essays on Native American Oral Literature.* Berkeley: University of California Press, 1983.

Swann, Brian, and Arnold Krupat, eds. *Recovering the Word: Essays on Native American Literature.* Berkeley: University of California Press, 1987.

Vizenor, Gerald (Ojibwa), ed. *Narrative Chance: Postmodern Discourse on Native American Indian Literatures.* Albuquerque: University of New Mexico Press, 1989.

Wiget, Andrew O. *Native American Literature.* Boston: Twayne, 1985.

————. *Critical Essays on Native American Literature.* Boston: G. K. Hall, 1985.

GLOSSARY

anthropology The study of the physical, social, and historical characteristics of human beings.

autobiography A life history of a person narrated by herself or himself.

biography A history of a person's life.

Bureau of Indian Affairs (BIA) A U.S. government agency now within the Department of the Interior. Originally intended to manage trade and other relations with Indians, the BIA today seeks to develop and implement programs that encourage Indians to manage their own affairs and to improve their educational opportunities and general social and economic well-being.

culture The learned behavior of humans; nonbiological, socially taught activities; the way of life of a group of people.

culture hero A mythical character who creates the world, provides resources and rituals humans need to survive, and defeats the enemies of humankind. Culture heroes are often tricksters who become the victims of their own mischievous pranks; their antics teach the consequences of improper behavior.

genre A category of artistic, musical, or literary composition characterized by a particular style, form, or content.

Ghost Dance movement A religious and cultural revival movement that spread among Indians in the 1890s and centered on the belief that non-Indians would disappear and the Indians' world would return if certain rituals were performed.

Indian Reorganization Act (IRA) The 1934 federal law that ended the policy of allotting plots of land to individuals and encouraged the development of reservation communities. The act also provided for the creation of autonomous tribal governments.

Indian Territory An area in the south central United States to which the U.S. government resettled Indians from other regions, especially the eastern states. In 1907, this area and Oklahoma Territory became the state of Oklahoma.

linguist A person who specializes in the study of human speech.

literature The body of works produced in a particular language, country, or age. Literature refers to both oral and written works.

myth A story of an event of the prehistoric past. Myths often explain a practice, belief, or natural phenomenon.

oral literature A body of literary works that are communicated verbally. Oral literature, which includes songs, stories, and ritual dramas, is sometimes called "verbal arts" or "folklore."

removal policy Federal policy that called for the sale of all Indian land in the eastern and southern United States and the migration of Indians from these areas to lands west of the Mississippi River.

ritual drama The term commonly used by scholars to refer to what Indians usually call chants, chantways, ceremonies, or rituals. Ritual dramas often combine song, narrative, and oratory.

INDEX

PICTURE CREDITS

Courtesy Paul Abdoo, page 100; Photograph courtesy of the Alaska State Museum, Juneau, page 55 (top); American Museum of Natural History, photo by Lee Boltin, page 26 (neg. # 2A 3634); AP/Wide World Photos, page 22; Archives and Manuscript Division of the Oklahoma Historical Society, pages 75, 86; Courtesy of the Bancroft Library, page 76; Courtesy Carolyn Barnes, page 96; © Jerry Bauer, page 94; Courtesy Michael Dorris, page 92; Courtesy Henry Holt & Co., page 90; Courtesy George Kew, page 88; Library of Congress, pages 19, 64, 72, 78; Courtesy Jay Miller, the Newberry Library, page 81; Minnesota Historical Society, page 31; Courtesy Museum of the American Indian, Heye Foundation, pages 29, 49, 56; The National Archives, page 83; Native American Painting Reference Library, Private Collection, pages 51 (top and bottom), 54; Nevada Historical Society, page 65; General research division, New York Public Library, Astor, Lenox and Tilden Foundations, pages 15, 41, 67; Courtesy the New York State Library, Albany, Manuscripts and Special Collections Division, page 45; Schoharie Museum of the Iroquois Indian, pages 47, 50; Smithsonian Institution, Department of Anthropology, page 38 (neg. # 31155-E); Smithsonian Institution, National Anthropological Archives, pages 12 (neg. # 55300), 25 (neg. # 82-2048), 35 (neg. # 55297), 58 (neg. # 2906), 68 (neg. # 4793); Special Collections Division, University of Washington Libraries, page 62 (neg. # NA 893); Courtesy United States Department of the Interior, Indian Arts and Crafts Board, Southern Plains Indian Museum, page 55 (bottom); UPI/Bettmann Archive, page 79; Reprinted from *The Way to Rainy Mountain* © 1969, University of New Mexico Press, pages 2, 43, 70; The Wheelwright Museum of the American Indian, pages 52–53 (cat. # P4-#4); Courtesy Irene Young, page 95.

Cover, Storyteller figurine by Helen Cordero, courtesy of Adobe Gallery, Albuquerque, NM. Photo by Focus Studio.

ACKNOWLEDGMENTS

Excerpt from "Digging Out the Roots" from *Digging Out the Roots* by Duane Niatum. Copyright © 1978 by Duane Niatum. Reprinted by permission of Harper & Row, Publishers, Inc.

Excerpt from "Dreams Children Had" from *La Plata Cantata* by Jim Barnes. Purdue University Press, Copyright © 1989 by Purdue Research Foundation, West Lafayette, IN 47907. Reprinted with permission.

Excerpt from "Grandma's Dying" from *Skins and Bones* by Paula Gunn Allen. Copyright © 1988 by Paula Gunn Allen. Reprinted by permission of West End Press.

Excerpt from "I Was Sleeping Where the Black Oaks Move" from *Jacklight* by Louise Erdrich. Copyright © 1984 by Louise Erdrich. Reprinted by permission of Henry Holt and Company, Inc.

Excerpt from "I think of the lights" from *My Horse and a Juke Box* by Barney Bush (Los Angeles: UCLA American Indian Studies Center, 1979). Reprinted by permission of the UCLA American Indian Studies Center.

Excerpt from "Plea to Those Who Matter" (a poem included in *Riding the Earthboy 40* by James Welch). Copyright © 1971 by James Welch. Reprinted with permission of Confluence Press at Lewis-Clark State College, Lewiston, Idaho.

A. LAVONNE BROWN RUOFF is professor of English at the University of Illinois at Chicago, where she developed the Native American Studies program. She has been named a fellow of the Institute of the Humanities of UIC for 1990–91.

In 1981, Dr. Ruoff was awarded a research grant from the National Endowment for the Humanities, for which she has conducted summer seminars on American Indian literatures for college teachers in 1979, 1983, and 1989. Among other distinctions she has received are a 1989 distinguished service citation from the Indian Council Fire for her work with the Indian community in Chicago and the 1986 award from the Society for Study of Multiethnic Literatures in the United States for her contributions to ethnic studies.

Currently, Dr. Ruoff is the general editor of the American Indian Lives series published by the University of Nebraska Press. She has also served as a member of the Modern Language Association's Commission on the Literatures and Languages of America (1980–83) and of the American Literature Committee, Fulbright Scholar Awards (1987–90), of which she was chairperson in 1989–90.

Her publications include *American Indian Literatures: An Introduction, Bibliographic Review, and Selected Bibliography* (1990) and the introduction and annotation of the 1987 reprint of *The Moccasin Maker*, a collection of short fiction by 19th-century Mohawk writer E. Pauline Johnson. She also has co-edited *Redefining American Literary History* (1990) and has written 26 book chapters and articles on Indian literatures.

FRANK W. PORTER III, general editor of INDIANS OF NORTH AMERICA, is director of the Chelsea House Foundation for American Indian Studies. He holds a B.A., M.A., and Ph.D. from the University of Maryland. He has done extensive research concerning the Indians of Maryland and Delaware and is the author of numerous articles on their history, archaeology, geography, and ethnography. He was formerly director of the Maryland Commission on Indian Affairs and American Indian Research and Resource Institute, Gettysburg, Pennsylvania, and he has received grants from the Delaware Humanities Forum, the Maryland Committee for the Humanities, the Ford Foundation, and the National Endowment for the Humanities, among others. Dr. Porter is the author of *The Bureau of Indian Affairs* in the Chelsea House KNOW YOUR GOVERNMENT series.